HOUSE LOVE

MOOR BAKER ARCHITECTS

HOUSE LOVE

TEXT BY CHRIS BAKER
INTRODUCTION BY PETER MOOR
STYLED BY MARY JUCKIEWICZ
PHOTOGRAPHY BY JESSICA KLEWICKI GLYNN

VENDOME
NEW YORK · LONDON

THIS BOOK IS DEDICATED TO THOSE WHO HAVE TAUGHT US BEST WHAT *HOUSE LOVE* IS—OUR OWN FAMILIES. FOR ALEX, EDDIE, JACK, HENRY, AND AARON

LESSONS FROM VERMONT

PETER MOOR

AFTER GRADUATING FROM ARCHITECTURE SCHOOL, MY WIFE, Mary, and I both found ourselves working in the heart of New York City's Upper West Side, just steps apart on Broadway. Mary was at 72nd Street in the now-demolished Colonial Club, while I worked at the stately Central Savings Bank Building at 74th Street. Each morning, we set out from our prewar apartment in Fort Greene, Brooklyn, convinced that the rest of our lives would unfold within the rich tapestry of New York City's urban landscape. The energy of the city, its rhythm and complexity, felt intrinsic to our identity as architects. We thought we were firmly rooted in this vibrant environment until an unexpected opportunity altered our path. Friends asked us if we would design a house for them in the mountains of southern Vermont. We accepted the commission, confident that Vermont would benefit from our urban sensibilities and a touch of New York sophistication. We envisioned bold, sleek, and urbane interventions. Lo and behold, our early schemes were met with a lukewarm reception. Our friends had something else in mind: a Vermont house. Determined to please them and meet their expectations, we paused to reflect: What, exactly, is a Vermont house?

The answer revealed itself not in theory but in the landscape itself: the dignified simplicity of weathered barns, the sturdy stone walls that traced the fields, and the homes that seemed to have grown organically from the earth. These were buildings of purpose and restraint, shaped by climate, materials, and tradition. Humbled and inspired, we dropped our swagger, embraced these lessons and traditions, and soon found ourselves embracing Vermont itself. Vermont embraced us in return. Drawn to the quiet beauty and enduring craftsmanship of the region, we left Brooklyn behind and settled in South Londonderry, Vermont.

Our new firm, River House Design, aptly took its name from our tiny house beside the West River. Our studio was in a converted garage on the property, its only heat source a woodstove. Every morning, I would rise early, coffee in hand, to light the fire—a small ritual that helped keep the cold at bay and allowed our work to unfold in comfort.

Our first Vermont project was well received, and in time, other commissions followed. As our practice grew, so did our connection to the place. We bought a mid-1800s Cape in Weston, Vermont, and moved our studio to the second floor of the Oddfellows Hall, a space that placed us at the heart of the town and community we had come to love.

With the arrival of our daughter—and a pair of sheep to complete the pastoral scene—we believed we had again found the place where we would spend the rest of our lives. Yet Vermont winters, as beautiful as they were, proved formidable. After we had endured several winters, a visit to Mary's parents in Florida offered a stark contrast. Something about the warmth, the light, and the help of family prompted another move. Occasional examples of thoughtful buildings and homes in Florida made it seem like a place where the ethos of Vermont, if applied, could bring wonderful results.

Before long, Mary and I opened shop again, and our roots began to take hold in the Florida sand. Our first commission was with a local builder who soon hired us to design his personal residence. That, in turn, led to additional commissions, including The Long View (see pages 183–203). It was this very home that inspired Chris Baker to join our firm more than twenty years ago, after touring it during her interview—a decision for which we remain profoundly grateful. We are deeply appreciative of these clients for commissioning us and for making their love for their home apparent.

We were fortunate to have Chris Baker in the firm. With her keen design sensibility, her grasp of tectonics, and her exceptional ability to foster relationships, she quickly became an indispensable part of our practice. Her leadership, coupled with her thoughtful approach to design, naturally led to her becoming a partner in the firm.

Recently, I had the pleasure of returning to Vermont with Chris. Revisiting our early projects—and collaborating on a new home in Manchester—reminded us of the values that have quietly guided our work across decades and landscapes: respect for place, for materials, for the enduring power of thoughtful design, and for the reward of clients loving their homes.

PRECEDING PAGES: Trying to look serious in front of our first residential commission, where we employed the wisdom and traditions of a simple Vermont house, completed in 1985.

OPPOSITE: Our daughter, free from the coats and hats and mittens but not the Vermont-esque gable ends, in front of the first house we built for ourselves in Florida, completed in 1991.

ABOVE: Our most recent Vermont house incorporates Japanese shou sugi ban (burnt wood) barn siding, completed in 2023.

OUR
HOUSE

PETER MOOR

OUR HOUSE, BUILT IN 2002, IS SITUATED FOUR LOTS IN FROM THE Atlantic on a dirt lane reminiscent of Old Florida. Mary Juckiewicz, my wife and partner at the firm, discovered it when she visited the lane to look at the work of two local artists who had a home and studio on an oceanfront lot. After her visit, she noticed an unoccupied wooded lot and, upon further investigation, found a FOR SALE sign face down and partially covered with vines and palm fronds. We went back to the lot later that day and were smitten. Soon it was ours, and we began the process of designing our own home, inspired by the vernacular styles of St. Augustine, Florida; Charleston, South Carolina; Vermont; and Windsor, a New Urbanist development just being built across town. We opted for a side-yard, upside-down scheme, locating the living and dining areas, kitchen, and primary bedroom on the second floor, where the sounds, breezes, and scents of the ocean are amplified. With the narrow, one-room-deep elevation facing the lane, the northern and southern sides of our forty-by-forty-foot courtyard are flanked by six-foot-tall walls and hedges. The courtyard connects the carport and garage on the eastern side to the two-story house on the western side. A motor court to the north of the courtyard keeps visitors' cars out of view, while a gate in the south courtyard wall leads to the walled, hedge-lined pool court. We certainly achieved house love, which we have enjoyed over the years. And now our grown children with their children cherish their return home.

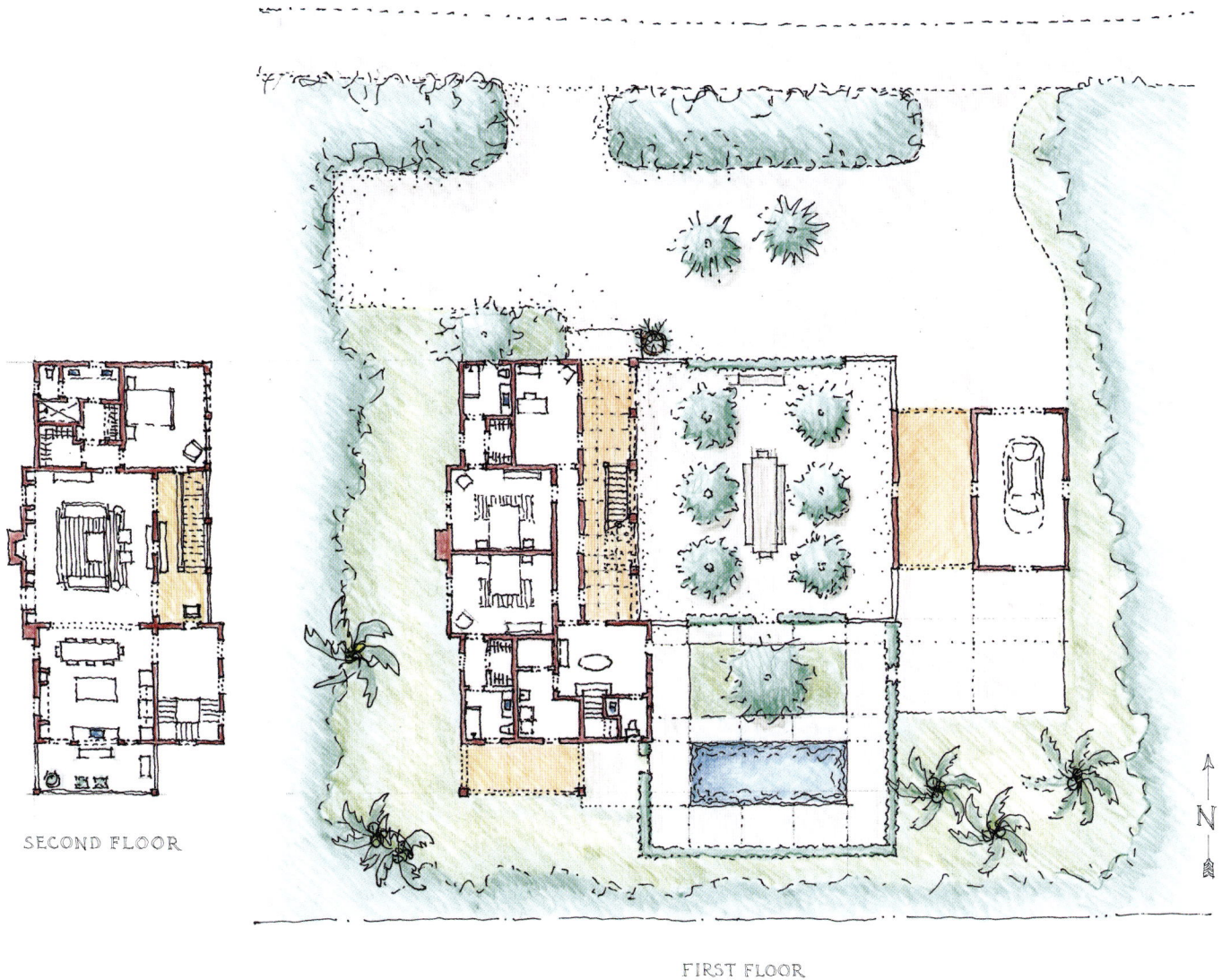

SECOND FLOOR

FIRST FLOOR

PAGE 18: The narrow gable and "shed" over the louvered porch facing the street say "house" with the simplicity of a child's drawing.

PAGES 20–21: Site walls and hedges share the chore of defining the pool court.

PRECEDING PAGES: Once you pass the louvers at the entrance, you can go straight or up, or just hang out on the porch.

OPPOSITE: The carport on the east side of the courtyard keeps our car away from view and the surfboards and Daisy in the shade.

ABOVE AND OPPOSITE: In the entry hall on the lower level, the flooring is terra-cotta tile. An old cypress return-air grille has been transformed into a display case for shells. The sculpture of a building is by local artist Gustaf Miller.

OPPOSITE: My painting of Belted Galloways in Rockport, Maine, is a reminder of cooler climes.

OPPOSITE: On the second level, an arched opening at the top of the stair frames the dining area, which is flanked by the kitchen and living room.

ABOVE LEFT AND RIGHT: Fronds, books, and sea beans—just a few of our favorite things.

RIGHT: Glassware on shelves in front of a west-facing window add sparkle to the kitchen cupboard.

BEAUTIFUL CHILDREN
TREE OF SMOKE
JOHN IRVING
BORROMINI
LOUIS SULLIVAN
ERNEST HEMINGWAY

PRECEDING PAGES: In the living room, a masonry fireplace lends both visual warmth and comfort on the occasionally chilly Florida night.

ABOVE: The view from the living room to the kitchen, where south-facing windows and a glass door look out on the treetops. Our children called the second floor the "monkey level."

OPPOSITE: Soapstone counters and backsplashes, face-frame cabinetry, and tall cupboards all have a Vermont kitchen sensibility.

OPPOSITE: Florida landscapes featuring the native cabbage palm by local artists: Sean Sexton (top and bottom left), René Guerin (top right), and me (bottom left.) The male and female bird renderings are the work of a local high school student. We love our rattan.

ABOVE: During the pandemic, we held our daughter's intimate wedding reception in the courtyard.

RIGHT: The courtyard, the biggest "room" in the house, is both festive and relaxing.

PRETTY

IN

PINK

BEING MISTAKEN FOR DEAD ARCHITECTS IS A COMPLIMENT FOR any committed classical architect. In this instance, however, one person knew better— the Realtor. A family new to Palm Beach had identified their favorite house on the island, a rambling, white, Bermuda-style home on a beachfront corner. They told their Realtor that they would hire the architects of that house if they were still alive. Luckily for us, we were.

Our clients wanted a new Old Palm Beach house for several reasons and asked us to assemble the right team. Peter once compared the feeling of a great team to that of a jazz band, or in this case a bluegrass band, and that's exactly what we put together. It took little time to find the builder, Tim Givens. He lived on the island, had no website, had started his career as a framing carpenter, and never missed a morning beach walk with his wife, who runs the office. Talented craftspeople surrounded him, and building beach houses felt like a side hustle to his full-time banjo gig. He had taken apart many old buildings in town, which happens to be the best way to learn what holds up and what feels good.

About the same time, we met interior designer Tom Scheerer. We had just discovered his first book, *Tom Scheerer Decorates*, admired every page, and felt that his style—sophisticated, practical, and not too serious—was perfectly suited to our clients. They loved his work and called him up. Of course, getting to work with Tom is not quite that easy, but after we sent along our plans, he was "in." We were delighted. The spaces were not small but not big either, and the rooms were somewhat separated from one another. Tom was the perfect collaborator— talented, direct, and after what was best for the project. The same can be said for landscape

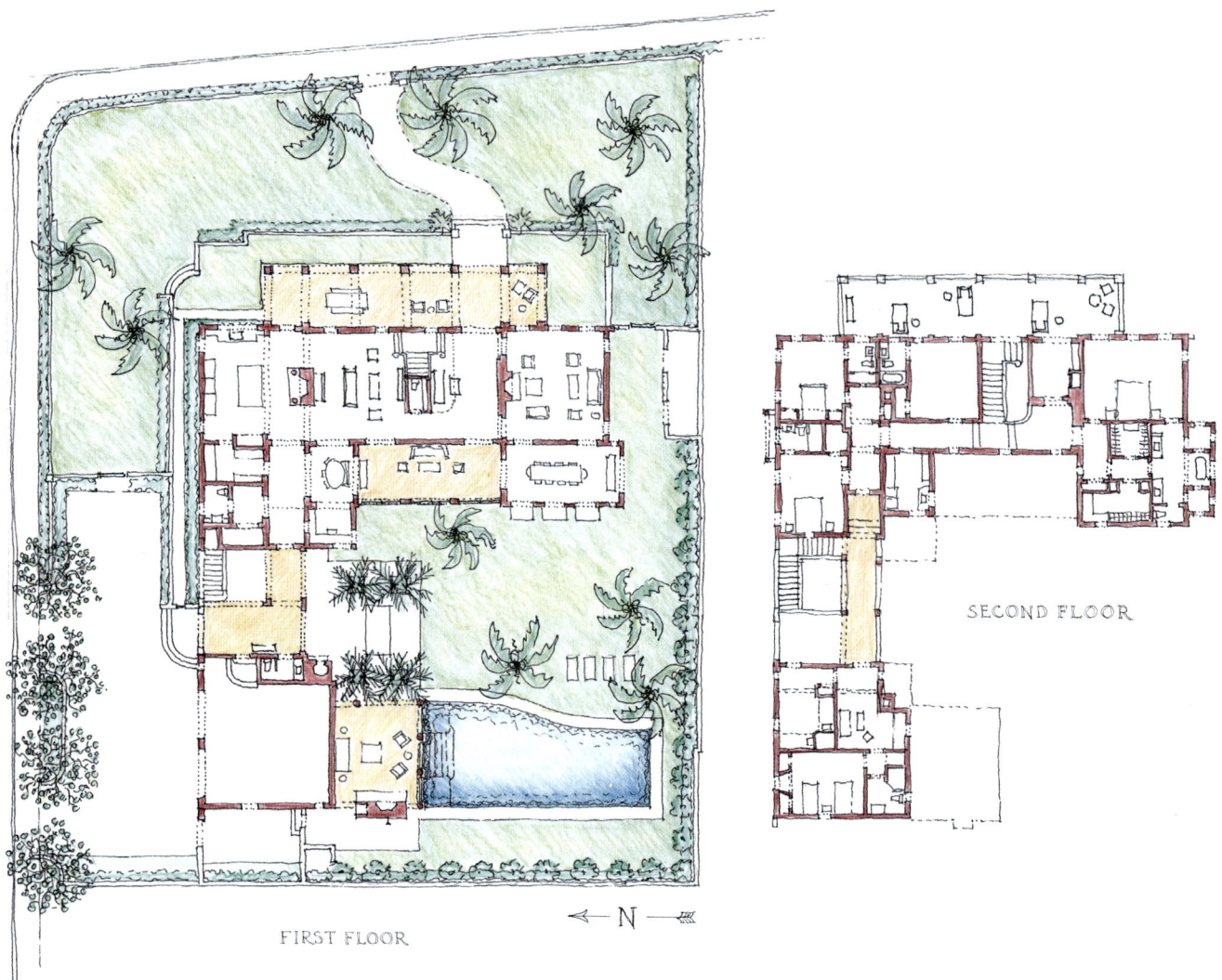

SECOND FLOOR

FIRST FLOOR

← N →

PAGE 40: Reading more like the icing on a cake than a highly functional roof, this white, thickly slurried roof is common in the tropics to deter rot and wind. Shadows accentuate the details: the hand-worked stucco, the thick wooden shutters and their "shutter dogs," and the brick windowsills.

PAGES 42–43: A low perimeter site wall and a stand of mature coconut palms keep the view of the house open as a friendly gesture to the neighborhood. Upstairs, the outdoor shower, cantilevered off the house to capture a view of the ocean, is visible to the left.

PAGE 45: The quirky, off-center front door in the six-bay porch was made of old-growth cypress, known for its tight, durable grain, by a local shop and fitted with bronze hardware from E. R. Butler. The Lyford sconce, designed by Tom Scheerer for The Urban Electric Company, is a Moor Baker favorite.

PRECEDING PAGES: Ping-Pong reigns supreme in this family, and a concrete Ping-Pong table is centered on the side entry. The main house and guesthouse are connected by an open-air, elevated breezeway, with an alfresco stair tucked just inside the arched opening.

OPPOSITE: A painted picnic table on the formal front porch reinforces the friendly spirit of this client. Above is the sleeping porch.

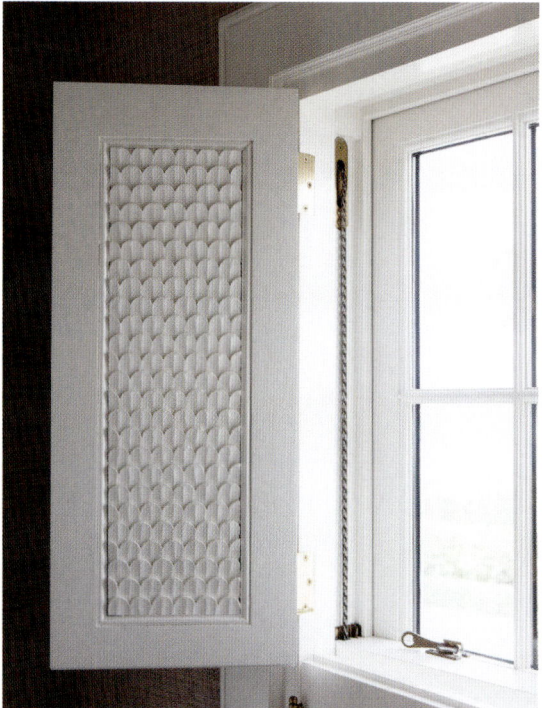

architect Mario Nievera. The gardens, house, and decorating were inseparable, developed in harmony, and all reinforcing the clients' initial dream.

The reason this couple wanted a "new" old house, rather than a new "new" house, was largely to avoid the mustiness that comes with air-conditioning a building that was never meant to be air-conditioned. Our charge was to eliminate not only that mustiness but also the "new-house smell" caused by the off-gassing of new materials. As it turns out, it is easier to avoid materials that off-gas by employing old-school methods of construction. We traded plywood glues and pressure-treated woods for Boral-dusted lumber, which happened to be turquoise in color. We installed antique oak flooring atop diagonal decking instead of conventional plywood, and we used wooden sleepers to raise the decking an inch above the concrete structural slab, ensuring a softer feel underfoot, as well as a creak or two. The framers were joyful, the framing was beautiful, and we all hated to cover it up. Linseed-oil finishes were practically edible, garden lime dusted the cypress porch ceilings, naturally repelling insects, and peppermint oil covered leaves in the garden for the same purpose. Tom rethought furnishings and fabrics, and Mario created a beautiful garden, knowing there would be no chemical pesticides to do the heavy lifting. The garden is a respite for birds and (only the cute) bugs, with hardy sod that is not always perfectly green in the winter but capable of taking a deep drink of water. Moor Baker may have conjured the overall vision of this home, but its soul was created by the entire team of designers and craftspeople, all of whom were fully committed to exploring our clients' desire for a healthy, handmade home.

OPPOSITE: We delighted in the handmade details of this house. *TOP ROW:* Necessary support expressed as haunches for porch framing; solid antique oak stair treads and shapely, profiled spindles; a working kitchen fireplace. *CENTER ROW:* A hand-carved teak shutter by The Raj Company unfolds over a traditional weight-and-chain-operated mahogany window; the thickly slurried roof coated in mineral paint deters mildew; bronze shutter dogs. *BOTTOM ROW:* Low-tech pivot hinges; tectonic shadows; encaustic-cement Cuban tiles in custom colorations are used liberally as a durable wallpaper throughout the interior.

PAGE 52: The most-used entrance off the breezeway. Etched-brass light switches by Forbes & Lomax sit below the less attractive pool-control panel, which is concealed behind a pair of hinged doors. The plaster ceiling is curved to accommodate the slope of the stair leading to the guest suites above.

PAGE 53: The view from the dining room of the living room and the Atlantic beyond. Gloss-painted pecky cypress ceilings brighten the rooms.

PAGES 54–55: A simple, shapely stucco fireplace anchors the living room. Just beyond it are the old-growth cypress front door (to the right) and the screened porch (to the left).

PAGES 56–57: The screened porch overlooks the backyard.

PRECEDING PAGES: Tom Scheerer surprised us by embellishing the plaster walls and ceiling of the dining room with faux-bamboo trim painted by Brian G. Leaver. The cement tile floor and narrow plaster moldings give this space the feel of an enclosed porch. Three pairs of arched French doors open into the backyard.

OPPOSITE: The breakfast room looks into the screened porch and is situated at the intersection of the kitchen, family room, and home office.

PRECEDING PAGES: Located in the northeastern corner of the house, the kitchen is a cheerful morning spot, flooded with natural light as the sun rises over the Atlantic.

OPPOSITE: A narrow but well-appointed back kitchen houses coffee, wine, smoothies, and an extra dishwasher to keep the kitchen less cluttered.

ABOVE: The kitchen sink boasts the best view in the house. Tall, playfully ventilated cupboards make access to tableware easy. The lightly wire-brushed, hand-painted cabinetry and woodwork make paint touch-ups a breeze.

OPPOSITE: The walls of the moody, light-filled office are painted the color of the Gulf Stream.

OVERLEAF LEFT: Oculus love. The primary bath has two showers, one of which is open to the elements and has clear views of the ocean across the street and the sky above.

OVERLEAF RIGHT: French doors, glazed with pastel-colored restoration glass, open into the primary bath, casting watercolor-like shadows, an idea inspired by a visit to Ca' d'Zan, winter home of the Ringling family in Sarasota, Florida.

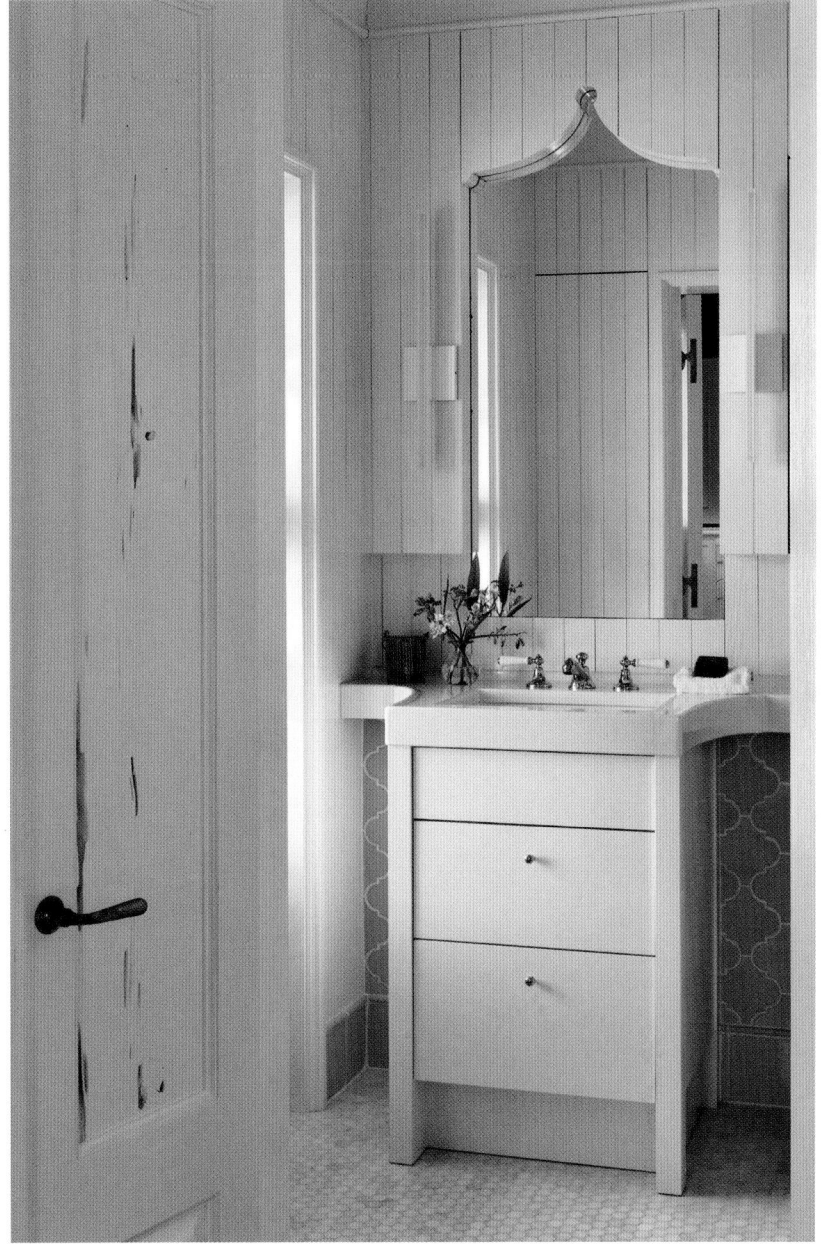

OPPOSITE: The bedroom suites are cozy and well-appointed. Wardrobes flank the bed, and a headboard shelf and niches replace traditional nightstands. Thickly painted, carved-teak shutters black out the light when closed—low-tech.

ABOVE LEFT AND RIGHT: The en suite bathroom opens onto the oceanfront sleeping porch. The custom lava-stone sink top was designed with rolled edges for easy cleaning. Small but commodious, the room accommodates the many sundries of teenage daughters, all tucked neatly away in cabinets behind the wall planking.

ABOVE: Three bunks in the guesthouse bedroom, equipped with cushions and bedrolls instead of mattresses and sheets, allow the space to double as a lounge. It's one of many functional moves to maximize the small spaces. Each of the bunks has a conveniently placed niche, a light switch, and drawers. A friend in Vero Beach leather-wrapped the metal bunk ladder, which was custom made by a Palm Beach marine shop.

OPPOSITE: The bathroom in the pool cabana is well equipped for wet swimmers. The sink, a single piece of glazed French lava stone, floats in a stucco surround. The perforated privacy screen is seen reflected in the mirror. The walls are clad in old-growth cypress.

LEFT: Looking into the pool courtyard from the elevated breezeway. Seaworthy materials are required for what we call "a boat that doesn't move." Here, the cypress ceiling is coated with a garden lime paste that makes it less appealing to insects. The railing, fashioned out of cut and painted bricks, is maintenance-free. Concrete posts are a more durable version of their wooden predecessors.

RIGHT: In this view of the pool courtyard, one can appreciate the piano curve of the pool coping, which is wide enough to accommodate a sunbather. The perimeter of the courtyard is richly layered for privacy, with the site wall fronted by a robust hedge. The dark brown trunks line up in a perfectly imperfect rhythm against the conch shell–pink stucco wall, an example of landscape architect Mario Nievera's artistry.

OVERLEAF: The cabana is sited right at the pool's edge, causing the dancing light from the water to be reflected on all surfaces, including a bas-relief reminiscent of a Matisse cutout, dreamed up by Scheerer and executed on-site by Frank Reijnen. The concrete columns were carefully formed and then poured in place. Out of sight is the dog wash and the outdoor shower, mounted on the back of the fireplace.

PAGES 80–81: The serpentine pool edge adds a few extra feet of lawn to accommodate chaise longues in front of the screened porch and dining room.

HORSE

PLAY

I N A FIRST FOR US, WE WERE ASKED TO DESIGN TWO HOUSES AT the same time by the same family, and with the same interior designer and landscape architect. We were a year or so into the design of "Pretty in Pink" with Tom Scheerer and Mario Nievera (see pages 40–81) when the clients saw images of Tom's house in the Bahamas and thought it might be a jumping-off point for the second home they had in mind. This family of equestrians had begun to wear a groove in the road between their beach house and the riding center and asked us to conjure up a weekend retreat west of town where they could kick off their boots.

The beach house and the house "out west" had different goals, the first of which was budget. That's not to say that one was better than the other—they were just different—and that was the great fun of it. Cost has little to do with a project's success. Knowing the budget from the outset is the trick. The same principles always apply: designing to the specific site, using materials that improve with age, accommodating a list of needs, and never skimping on charm. The second goal for the weekend house was to create something practical and durable, a home base to relax in after strenuous days at the equestrian center.

The lot, perhaps the last one available in the neighborhood, was an odd shape due to its location on a bustling, very visible corner. We quickly discovered two wonderful features: its perimeter of mature oak trees and its very narrow building setbacks. These features enabled us to design a perfect courtyard house. We threw the rooms into the centrifuge and watched as four little structures spread out, pressing themselves against the trapezoidal lot's perimeter, tucked

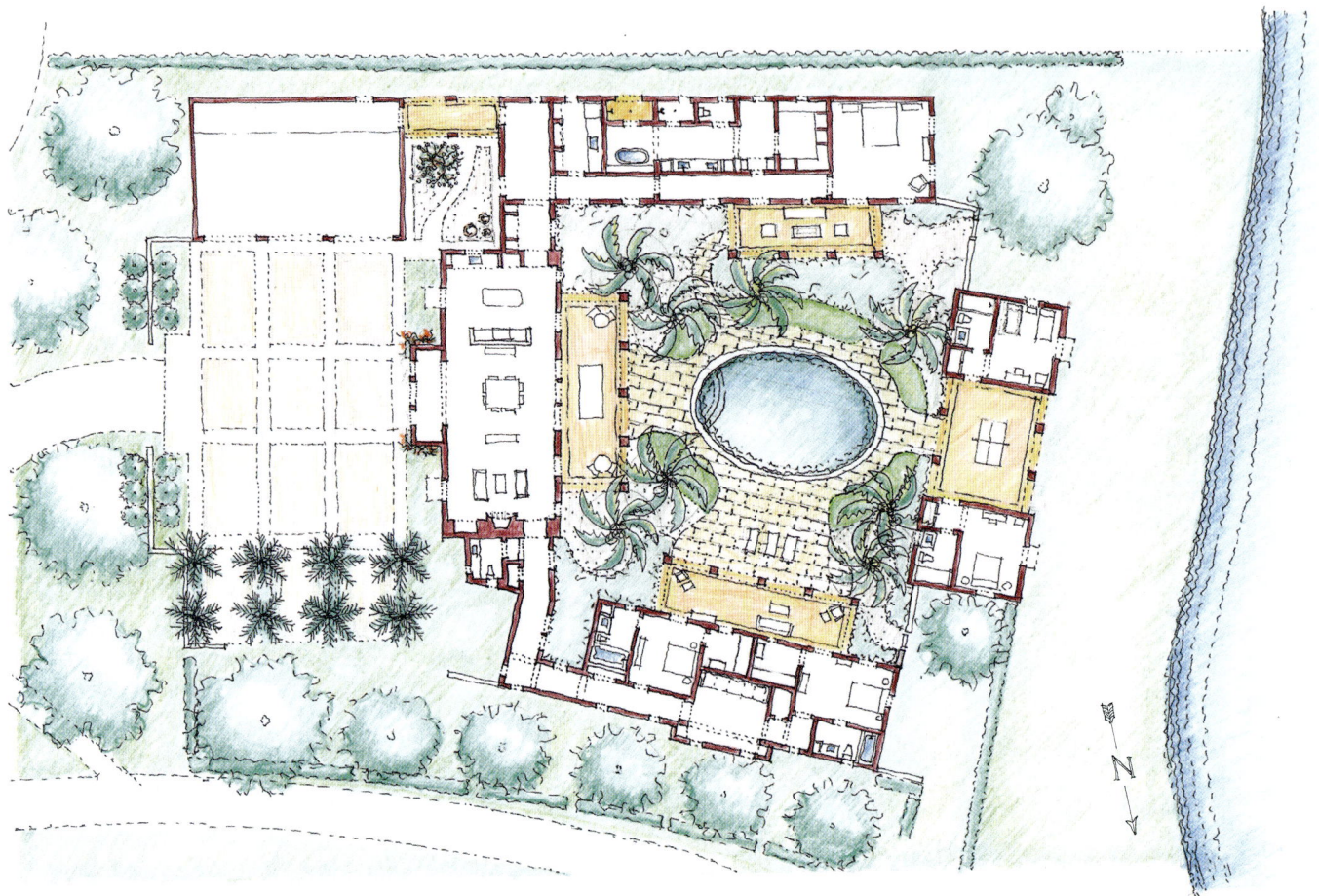

PAGE 82: A common native plant, a sea grape here trained into a tree, terminates a long interior axis from the primary bedroom and shades the path to the garage.

PAGES 84–85: A generous motor court of stained, brick-shaped pavers crisscrossed with shell stone welcomes guests.

PAGES 86–87: None of the existing perimeter oaks had to be moved, and their continuous canopy inspired the courtyard's design. Louvered shutters offer privacy from the street. The chainsawed-cedar sculpture in the foreground is *Wild Boar* by Marsia Holzer.

PRECEDING PAGES: In the entry hall, simple interior detailing, rounded plaster edges, a walnut travertine floor, and creamy white walls provide a serene backdrop for Scheerer's practical and beautiful furnishings.

OPPOSITE: The light-filled interiors all wrap around the central courtyard. Here, the dining table looks out on the dining porch, the raised pool, and the guest cabana's Ping-Pong porch.

up under the oak trees. As a result, a completely private courtyard was formed. A raised, oval pool in the center sits comfortably within the property's irregular geometry and, in a pinch, doubles as a watering trough, should a pony wander in.

We exercised restraint, using acres of the same materials throughout: huge pieces of brushed, walnut-colored travertine for the floors, flashes of chocolate- and chalk-glazed tiles, weathered cypress for interior doors, cabinets, and shutters, and a bit of leather wrapping on interior door levers for a softer feel.

It was great fun jumping back and forth between the beach house and this horsey place for a year or two, using perhaps a different set of brushes to paint each of them, but ending up with two great houses perfectly suited to the family.

OPPOSITE: The main living area occupies the tallest structure, anchored by a simple stucco fireplace. A narrow, window-lined hallway leads toward the guest bedrooms. The shutters are lightly wire-brushed cypress, a wood we used throughout the interior in a variety of ways.

OVERLEAF: A freestanding, cypress-clad wall separates the living area from the kitchen. The black stove pipe eliminates range exhaust. The hallway beyond leads to the bar, laundry room, garage, and primary suite.

OPPOSITE AND ABOVE: On the far side of the freestanding wall, durable materials handle a bustling kitchen with ease: glazed tiles, an enameled hood, brass shelving, honed black granite countertops, a thick slab of Carrara marble atop the island, and wire-brushed cypress cabinetry.

ABOVE: A chevron-patterned door opens into the powder room. The door's simple Baldwin lever is wrapped in leather to soften the feel.

RIGHT: The hall between the daughters' bedrooms widens into a cozy lounge. The oversize sofa, which doubles as a place for friends to sleep over, was made to fit. Carved shutters, inset with caning, darken the room for TV watching.

OVERLEAF LEFT: A soaking tub looks out into the narrow but lush side garden.

OVERLEAF RIGHT: The primary bath has an efficient but commodious galley layout. To one side, a long double vanity with ample drawers for sundries; to the other, the shower and water closet. A pitched ceiling adds loft to the narrow space.

OPPOSITE AND ABOVE: The daughters' bedrooms open onto a shared porch facing the courtyard. The rooms are small, but raised ceilings add volume. Scheerer is expert in furnishing small rooms to live large. We learned a few tricks that we now employ in our own homes.

ABOVE: The pool is the focal point of all four structures that surround it and add life to the courtyard.

OPPOSITE: The dining porch, outfitted with a narrow table and cushioned benches, easily accommodates many friends, a common occurrence during the equestrian season.

OVERLEAF: The low-maintenance garden of gravel, agave, coconut palms, and many native plantings is easily managed and can evolve over time, supervised by Mario Nievera as well as the family's trusted organic gardener, who also grows much of their food on their nearby farm.

PAGES 108–9: Separate guest bedrooms flank the Ping-Pong porch and screen the courtyard from view.

SHORE
BIRD

THIS PROJECT IN VERO BEACH, FLORIDA, SITS ON A LONG, OCEAN-front lot in Old Riomar, one of the most charming, walkable, and well-established neighborhoods in town. The owners requested a beach house for two, inspired by their Pennsylvania roots. One of the owners acted as her own decorator, a not uncommon occurrence for us, and an excellent shopper, often sharing photos of her most recent finds. For our first meeting, or perhaps the second, she arrived at our office with two things in tow: a handful of pastel hydrangeas and a big cardboard box filled with an old canvas tarp. The colors became touchstones throughout the project, and the tarp became a continual source of intrigue. It was actually a hand-painted backdrop from a play that she and her mother had rescued from a consignment-shop window display in Maine years earlier. The scale of it was monumental, and we often wondered where this unwieldy treasure so dear to her heart would wind up, never guessing its home would be front and center, lining the walls of the main stair hall.

The height of oceanfront homes above sea level is prescribed by FEMA these days. Meeting it can be a daunting challenge, but if thoughtfully considered, can add charm—and if you are lucky, a rare Florida basement. The drive leading to the house rises through the dappled light of an oak-tree and palm-frond canopy and arrives at a generous brick-paved motor court, where visitors have a choice of entrances. Straight ahead, the side door welcomes old friends who might leave a note on the Pennsylvania slate chalkboard just inside. To the left, carriage doors open to a workshop with a guest apartment above and, yes, a basement below.

SECOND FLOOR

FIRST FLOOR

←— N —→

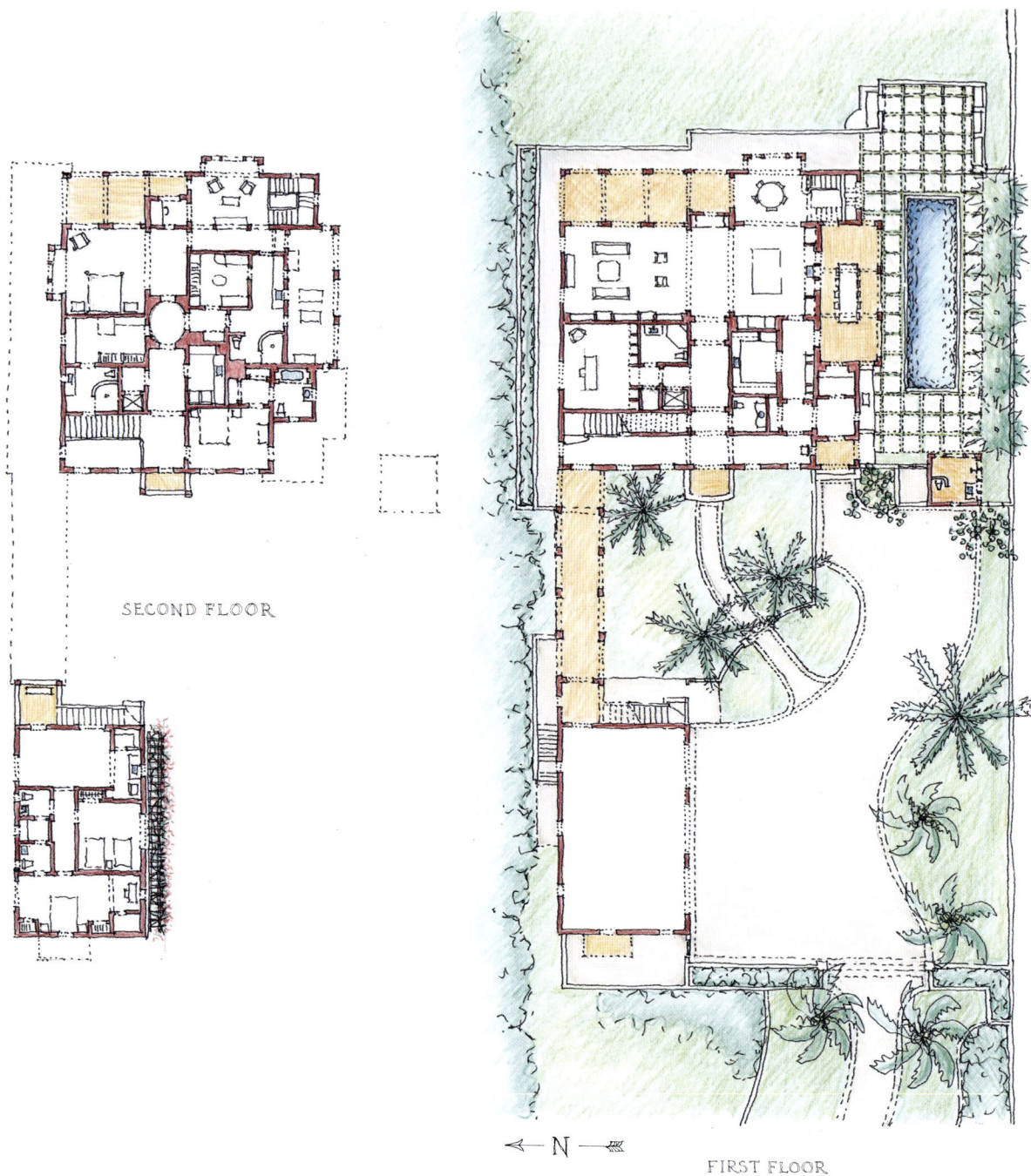

PAGE 110: The carriage house, doubling as a workshop, connects to the main house via a breezeway. The open roof framing exposes the underside of cedar shingles.

PAGES 112–13: Arriving at the brick-paved motor court, visitors have a choice of entrances. The building's plan has been layered, seemingly over time, with asymmetrical elements covering the points of entry.

PRECEDING PAGES: Medjool date palms shade the path to the lavender front door.

OPPOSITE: A harsh climate is the best editor. Brick, stucco, wood shingles, and tabby concrete all age gracefully in view of the ocean. The alfresco carriage-house stair leads to the guest apartment.

The alfresco carriage-house stairs offer a peek of the ocean before you duck into the apartment. For first-time visitors, there is also the front door through the formal entry court or the side gate, if they're ready to hit the pool. All nice choices to have.

At first blush, the floor plan might seem compact, more like a cozy, inward-focused, cold-weather home. This organization is a departure from our usual one-room-deep approach to architecture in the subtropics—the easiest way to ensure maximum natural light and cross breezes. In this case, we were challenged to provide an equivalent amount of light and breeze in a different way. When experienced in three dimensions, our solution becomes clear. Lofty, eleven-foot ceilings, nine-foot interior doors with transoms, and tall windows allow natural light to fill every room, despite the dense plan. The main stair hall is gracious; stretching the entire width of the front façade, it is flooded with light and affords views of the courtyard. From site plan to cabinet knobs, the project is certainly a portrait of this charming couple, who started out as clients and have become dear friends.

OPPOSITE: Just inside the side door, a Dutch door screens the laundry room from view, while a coconut-palm motif laser-cut into the top half of it affords a peek of the ocean.

OVERLEAF LEFT: Painted-brick floors and walls clad in wide horizontal beadboard planks create a beachy backdrop for straw hats and bags.

OVERLEAF RIGHT: The back stair connects the kitchen with the primary suite above. The window offers another framed peek of the water.

PRECEDING PAGES: A mirrored wall behind lacy wood fretwork reflects the view through the windows on the opposite wall, creating the illusion that there are ocean views along both sides of the living room. The stamped-metal air-conditioning grilles and light fixtures are incorporated into the built-in cabinetry.

OPPOSITE: The center hall, on axis with the Atlantic Ocean, frames a "picture" of the water through a single window in this inviting reading nook.

ABOVE: Planks of eastern white pine, sometimes as wide as eighteen inches, cover most of the floors, including the kitchen, seen here. Their softness takes the dings, dimples, and scratches of daily life, developing a lived-in patina that improves each year.

OPPOSITE: The back kitchen, housing the espresso machine and supplies, keeps the main kitchen tidy.

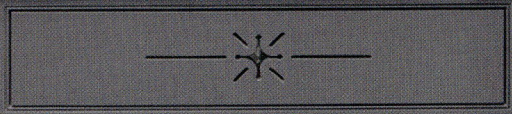

OPPOSITE: Late in the project, the main stair hall became the obvious home for an old theater backdrop of great sentimental value that the owner and her mother had found years ago in a consignment-shop window. We designed every last detail of the stair and millwork and had it made in town by our longtime local collaborators, Shaver Millwork.

OVERLEAF LEFT: Her bath borrows light and views from the sunporch; mirrored doors provide privacy.

OVERLEAF RIGHT: The guest bath, tucked under the roof framing, is just tall enough. The same wide pine floorboards used elsewhere are here painted a bright coral.

PRECEDING PAGES: Bathed in sunlight, the narrow, south-facing yard is perfect for our sun-loving clients. Its poured-in-place concrete elements are impervious to salt, sun, and sand.

OPPOSITE AND ABOVE: An outdoor pool cabana is both open to the elements and private. It features open roof framing, a tabby concrete floor, "windows" crisscrossed with cut and painted brick, and a hand-painted porcelain sink.

OVERLEAF: Shutters control light and airflow, ensuring comfort and a way to close up the porches during storm season. We often opt for handmade and hand-painted aluminum shutters, rather than wood, thanks to local artisans like Florida Shutters Inc., who continually refine their craft.

UNDER THE OAKS

THIS HOUSE TELLS THE STORY OF A QUINTESSENTIAL RELATIONSHIP between client and architect, one that spans most of Peter's career in Vero Beach. The deep, mutual admiration that this client and Peter have for each other's talents make the discussions between them something like a dance. For those of us lucky enough to have observed them, it has been a lesson in the beautiful innovations that often result from differences of opinion. What was once a working relationship has become a long-lasting friendship and, needless to say, she and Peter make great houses together.

This house, the second of three they have collaborated on, is situated on what most would identify as a dirt road, but to us locals, it is known as a sand road. The soft sand is reinforced with a mixture of pulverized shells, calcium, and lime. The lumps and bumps slow travelers, affording them time to look up and marvel at the main attraction, the Southern live oaks. These majestic trees are hundreds of years old and boast the widest of all oak canopies, which spread completely over the sandy lanes. With branches gnarly and twisted, they are products of their windswept environment, just a block from the Atlantic. They thrive in the salty air, blistering sun, and hurricane-force winds—elements that destroy a great many other things. And in their strength, they create a delicate shield, assuring safe harbor below—breezy, cool, and dappled in light. They are nature's perfect shade structures.

For the handful of fortunate residents living beneath them, a healthy reverence for the trees is essential. Our client's appreciation of her live oaks ran deep, so much so that our charge was to create a home amid them. It sounded simple enough, but upon closer inspection we realized

PAGE 138: A simple gate opens into a garden filled with Vero Beach's most iconic tree, the live oak. Hundreds of years old, their twisted trunks are a testament to their hardscrabble life near the windy shore.

PAGES 140–41: This home comprises a series of one-story jewel boxes meandering among the existing live oaks. A gravel motor court and antiqued terra-cotta roofs don't mind the leaves.

PAGE 142: Surrounding an alfresco fireplace, darkened-copper lanterns, steel-framed doors, and paving of coral stone accented by Old Chicago brick age gracefully.

PRECEDING PAGES: Our goal was to make it appear as if the trees had grown up around the house, not the other way around. The jewel-box quality of the structures is more obvious from the backyard.

OPPOSITE: A gravel path leads to the front door, located off-center from the main room.

just how many limbs and roots needed to be considered while planning the layout. Fortunately for us, the design gods cooperated, and not a single oak had to be moved (yes, you can move them) or removed. Just one root taunted us, but our local structural magician, Frank Farley, found a creative solution. He fashioned the foundation of the cabana building as a concrete bridge that spanned the obstreperous root, which now exists obliviously beneath the cabana.

Practicing for so many years in one place, we have learned who the local magicians are, and there is perhaps no better example than Sam Comer. The longtime owner of a landscape-installation business, Sam is humble, always supervising, coordinating, and finessing, so much so that it's easy to forget what a gifted designer he is. For us, the landscape and the architecture are inseparable, and we represent both in our first design sketches. In those early sketches, we compose gardens with a broad brush, indicating texture, scale, and color, and organize them more formally near the architecture. Sam, on the other hand, uses a much finer brush; though he's always deferential to our vision, his talents reside squarely at the intersection between practicality and beauty. And as this book is about house love, it's worth mentioning that Sam and his wife live in a house that we renovated years ago, a place now filled with his musings, our favorite of which might be his habitat for painted buntings. Shy birds with dramatic impact, it is no surprise that they are drawn to our friend Sam.

Our client was her own decorator, and like all the best decorators, she has an innate sense of scale rooted in comfort. Each room has just the right proportions for its function without overwhelming the person washing dishes or enjoying the fire. There is no formal front door; instead, a humble gravel path leads to a modest door in a left-of-center, completely glazed gallery. Inside, pecky cypress covers most surfaces, almost as a wallpaper might. Most people either love pecky or don't understand it at all. We find it charming, but it's really just a wood that's been attacked by a fungus, considered a castoff in the days before Florida's boom era.

OPPOSITE: The side door is a shortcut to the kitchen. A porch offers a bit of cover in the rain. We used pecky cypress for all porch ceilings and exterior rafters.

OVERLEAF: In the living room, located in the main jewel box, or pavilion, the walls are completely clad in pecky cypress. We had intended to paint the walls but stopped after the first coat of primer for a softer, more natural feel.

My grandmother used to say that nothing ever really dries in Florida, and she's right. Combine that fact with the abundance of seasonal leaves and pollen that drops from our beloved live oaks, and it can prove difficult to maintain a property here unless you choose your materials wisely. There are a handful of materials that do improve with age yet require minimal supervision, and we use them in a variety of ways. One of the Southern architects we admire most, the late A. Hays Town, described this casual maintenance plan as "benign neglect." Think of it as a patina that hurts nothing but the pocketbooks of power-washing companies. For this house, we employed curved terra-cotta roof tiles, a mineral paint over stucco, Spanish-cedar shutters, painted-steel window frames and doorframes, and large expanses of crushed-shell gravel. The house is a haven for our client, for passersby on the sandy lane, and for the moss and tiny plants living happily in the pitted coral stone underfoot.

PRECEDING PAGES: A glazed hall connects the living room to the dining room beyond, with the kitchen just around the corner. The floors throughout are a weathered Jerusalem limestone.

OPPOSITE: Hidden behind pecky cypress doors, the bar, clad from top to bottom in antiqued mirror, and its window overlooking the garden are a surprise.

ABOVE: The owner's collection of antique plates followed her from the last house we designed together.

RIGHT: The kitchen, open to a glazed porch, is as inviting as it is functional. Hand-painted terra-cotta tiles covering the walls and perimeter countertops lend an Old World charm. Take your dough and rolling pin to the limestone kitchen island.

ABOVE LEFT: One of the guest bedrooms is bathed in the afternoon glow.

ABOVE RIGHT: The gracious primary bath is reflected in the antique mirrored wall behind the vanity.

LEFT: Another guest bedroom.

OPPOSITE: Painted terra-cotta tiles cover the powder room. The clean-lined limestone sink was made for us in town.

OVERLEAF: The pool cabana doubles as a guesthouse, a comfortable place to stay for a good long while.

PAGES 162–63: The view from the cabana of the lap pool and live oak–lined lawn. Washed-cedar shutters modulate the breeze.

GOOD

NEIGHBOR

OUR "UNDER THE OAKS" CLIENT (SEE PAGES 139–63) COLLABORATED with us on this project just a few years later. Her own home, fondly described as a glassy jewel box, looks out onto her oak-canopied lane and directly faces the house across the street, so when the opportunity arose to purchase that property, she jumped at it. This was a chance to create "house love" for her future neighbor while enhancing her own.

Developing the lot started with an expedition to uncover the spectacularly mature sea grapes, oaks, and palms buried in the brush. The landscape design was an exercise in careful subtraction, and what was left still qualified as a formidable jungle. Local landscape designer Jane McBride understood the intention of the team well, refining the gardens with a light touch.

In the clearing we placed two structures, facing each other with a formalized garden in between—a welcome contrast to the surrounding jungle. The main building is a long rectangular structure, or "bar," with an equally long porch stretching along one side, the short end of which is gated and serves as the front door, a nod to the traditional side-yard houses of the South. The second structure is the garage, connected to the main house by way of a covered breezeway, ensuring dry passage to the main house while bifurcating the formal garden into two distinct areas.

At the entrance, a pleasant foyer leads to a hallway that extends in two directions. To the right are the kitchen and a cozy sitting room that seems to be ensconced in the garden. To the left is a light-filled, one-and-a-half-story great room, where a stair ascends to the second-floor bedrooms. We mitigated the scale of the great room's height by adding large, exposed

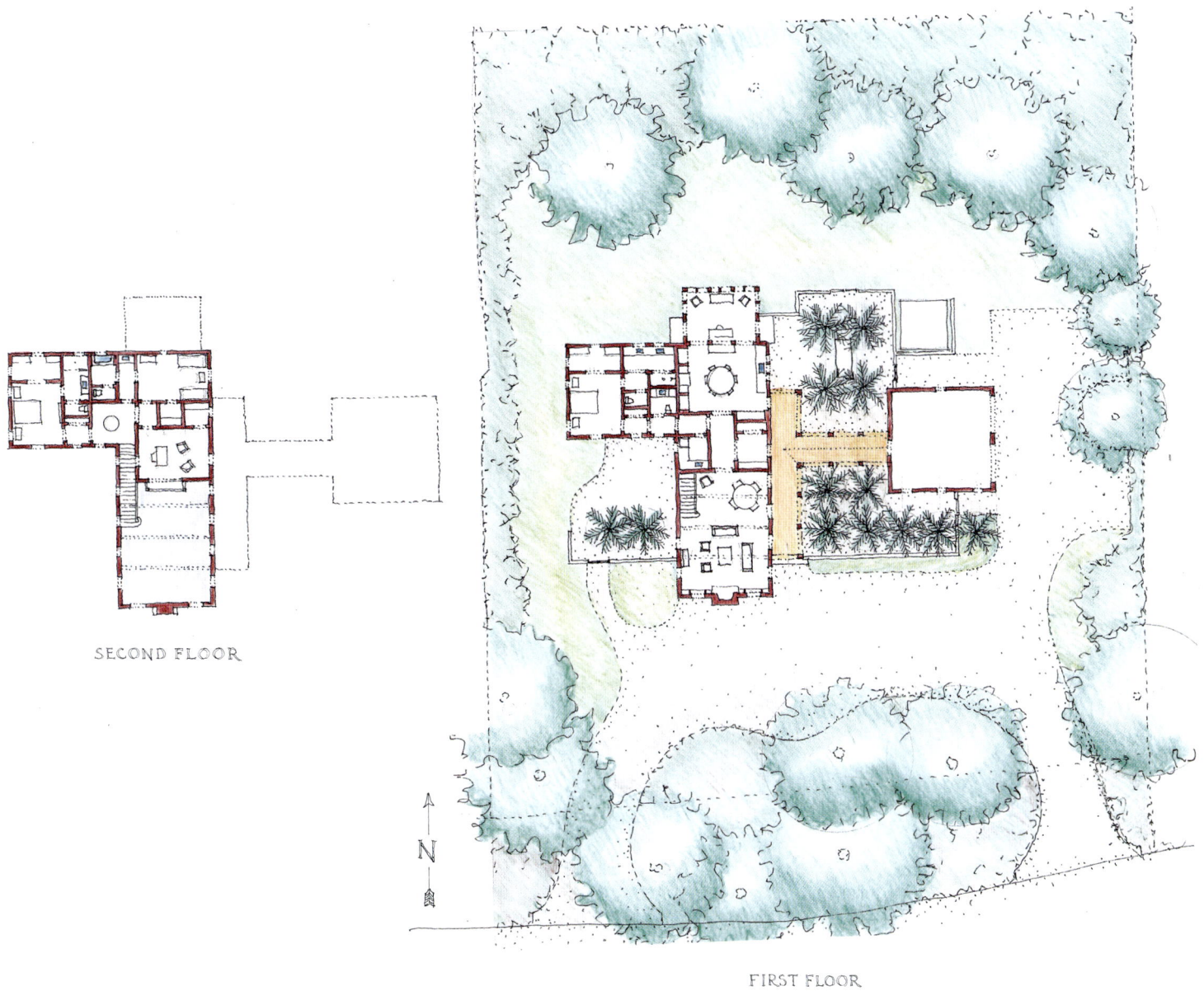

SECOND FLOOR

FIRST FLOOR

N

PAGE 164: A low gate, painted a chimichurri green, leads to the front door. Behind it, a series of covered porches connect the main house to the garage.

PAGES 166–67: The use of simple, durable materials were key to achieving sensible tropical charm. The wood-framed second story stays high and dry perched atop the stucco first-floor walls—a lesson borrowed from the St. Augustine, Florida, playbook.

PRECEDING PAGES: Sister houses on a sandy lane. A glimpse of our client's "Under the Oaks" house (see pages 139–63) can be seen from the front porch of this house, which she commissioned us to build as a speculative venture.

OPPOSITE: More functional than formal, the foyer leads into the hall between the kitchen and the great room.

trestles that span the upper reaches of the room. Suspended from them are large, darkened-brass light fixtures. We clad the walls in chunky framing lumber, which we left undressed and coated thickly with paint. We designed the stair and landing railings in a stylized Chippendale pattern. The stair treads are thick blocks of oak, again not overly worked. This client shares our penchant for quirky New England cottages, here charmingly exemplified by the dramatic change in scale between the soaring great room and the three cozy bedrooms upstairs.

Outside, beyond the formally landscaped courtyard, the garden is intentionally unstructured, looking as though it has always been there. The house is modest, gently placed in its surroundings, and thoughtful in its presentation to the street—a good neighbor.

OPPOSITE: To ensure that the great room's soaring ceiling did not preclude comfort, we layered the space: deep trusses and six large chandeliers fill the upper reaches; the wainscot extends three-quarters up the walls; bookcases at half the height of the room line the perimeter; and inviting upholstered window seats flank the woodburning fireplace.

OVERLEAF LEFT, TOP: A view through the kitchen into the glazed sunporch and out to the jungle beyond. The island is a table, designed by us and built by a local cabinet shop, along with the cabinetry.

OVERLEAF LEFT, BOTTOM, AND OVERLEAF RIGHT: The railings of the stair and bedroom balcony, made of framing lumber, are designed in a stylized Chippendale pattern. We eschew recessed downlights, preferring wall-mounted or hanging lights, which are equally bright and superior in charm. The hexagonal cement tile flooring by ARTO is cool and durable, and adds texture.

ABOVE: Chimichurri-green cabinetry echoes the shutters outside, and the tropical-patterned tile brings the dense landscape right into the kitchen.

OPPOSITE: The window above the kitchen sink overlooks the outdoor dining room.

OVERLEAF: This glassy sitting room is surrounded by the garden on three sides; the fourth side is partially open to the kitchen. It's the perfect place to tuck away out of the fray.

PAGES 180–81: Delineated by four palm trees and paved with tightly packed shell and coquina gravel, the outdoor dining room is one of two formal garden rooms in the space between the main house and the garage, separated by the breezeway. Ordinary materials are elevated simply by their arrangement and scale. The porch floor is poured concrete, its surface textured by sprinkling rock salt (used on icy roads up north to prevent slipping) over them while curing, and its edge dressed with Old Chicago brick. The "tin" roofs of the porch and breezeway act like a drum, turning summer rains into meditative sound, their undersides and the hand-framed rafters exposed.

THE
LONG
VIEW

PAGE 182: In site, plan, and character, this arts and crafts–inspired subtropical manor house perfectly matches the owners' sensibilities.

PRECEDING PAGES: Majestic native live oaks frame the front entry and gracious gravel motor court.

OPPOSITE: Visitors find this stand-alone guesthouse hard to leave.

ABOVE: The main house's steeply pitched slate roofs shed the oak leaves and Florida rains, while its smooth stucco walls, steel-framed windows, and shutters withstand the storms.

"THE LONG VIEW" DESCRIBES THIS PROJECT BOTH PHYSICALLY
and figuratively. The view from the house is in fact long, but the project's place in our
firm's history is even longer, as it influenced our beginnings in Florida and continues to inspire
our practice today. The plans for this house were likely the last to be completely hand-drawn
in our office; however, their concision, rigor, and spirit have informed the way we compose our
computer-assisted plans to this day. In fact, a copy of those plans is often the first thing waiting
on the seat of a newly hired member of our team—a perfect way to set the tone of what's to come.

Peter met and became friends with this dear Bostonian family more than thirty years ago.
A few years after that, they were ready to trade the challenges of oceanfront living for a tranquil
spot along the Indian River Lagoon and, much to young Peter's surprise, called on him to
design it. The long spit of land they purchased came to a point, and in a rather unconventional
move, Peter sited the house facing that lush point, rather than the water. Instead, angled,
glass-walled wings capture the water views. Formality was preferred, but playfully composed,
inspired by the nineteenth-century English homes and gardens of Sir Edwin Lutyens, Gertrude
Jekyll, and the like. The landscape became wilder the farther away it was from the architecture.
Broad swaths of ferns under the oaks, Sundown bougainvillea soaking up western light, and the
oval reflecting pool for swimming were all thoughtfully composed in collaboration with landscape architect Elizabeth Gillick. Inside, Peter collaborated with Lee Bierly and Chris Drake,
the family's decorators, also out of Boston. Lee was thoughtfully spontaneous and, like us, loved
to draw. They would trade sketches back and forth until they "had it," often in the presence

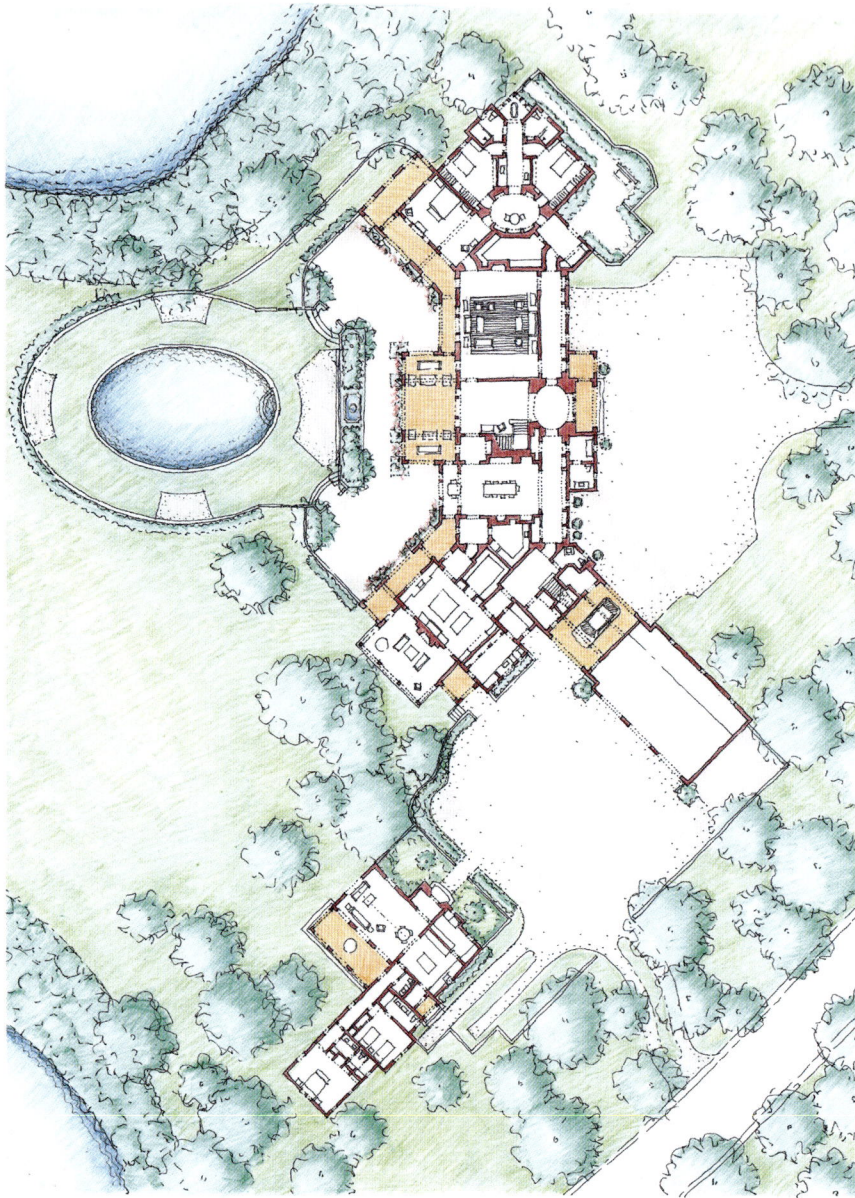

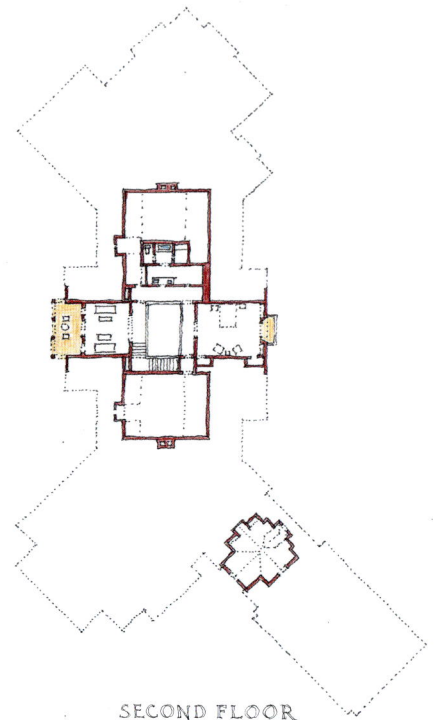

SECOND FLOOR

FIRST FLOOR

⫸ N →

PRECEDING PAGES: The entry hall finds itself on the long axis that runs from the oak-lined motor court in front to the oval pool at the rear. Pecky cypress on the ceiling, plaster walls, and ironwork railings all evoke Old Florida.

OPPOSITE: The west end of the front gallery leads from the kitchen to the primary suite. Wax softens the cast-stone floors over time; rounded plaster edges soften the light. Antiques abound, adding "soul," or, as our client would say, "a few whiskers."

of the clients. It was an exquisite collaboration and the kind of graphic communication that continues to prevail in our studio today.

The project was a success, the friendship endured, and a few years later I walked through the door of what was then Moor & Associates. I had moved to Florida to follow my heart, then struggled to find my place. Back then, moving to Florida was far less glamorous than it is now, garnering an inquisitive look at best. The day we met, Peter drove me to The Long View. I was completely charmed, eager to learn how to arrange bricks and sticks in such a compelling way. What I would discover were those same "Vermont lessons" that Peter and Mary had learned years before: beauty comes from solving problems unique to each place, using materials well suited for the job. Here, the sweeping roof lines were not only dramatic but also deflected rainwater. The deep carriage-door overhangs were both lovely and designed to protect the doors from moisture and too much sun. This functional approach to creating beauty is what makes our job as architects never finished; we are always learning from the past so we can better shape the future.

OPPOSITE: A walled side garden with Florida keystone paving opens off the primary suite.

OVERLEAF: In the comfortably formal living room, we employed many of the same materials as in the entrance hall, including the pecky cypress ceiling, plaster walls, and steel-framed doors and windows by Hope's. We find that the use of similar materials throughout a home establishes continuity and lends a sense of calm.

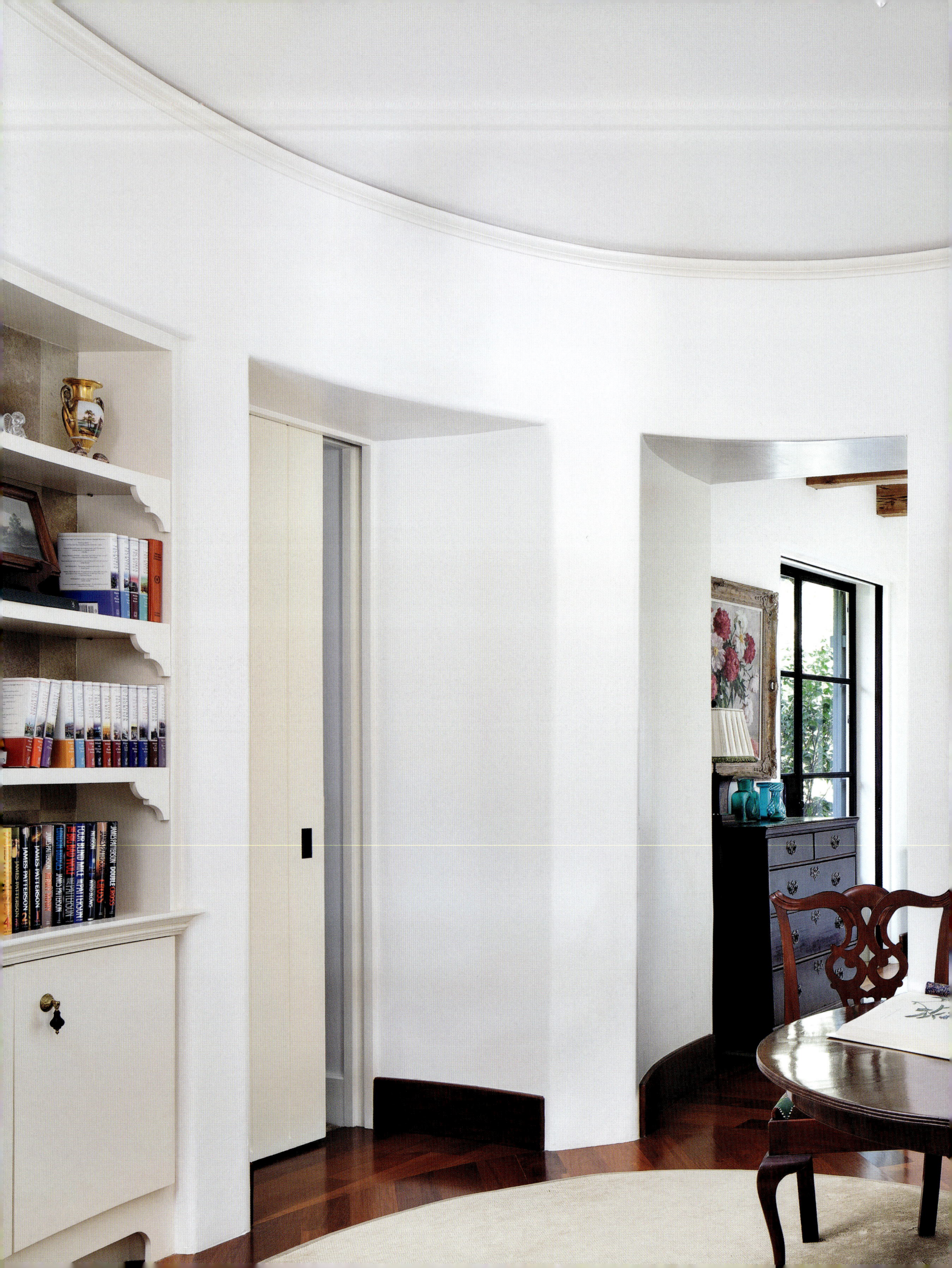

FREDERICK FORSYTH

THE FOURTH PROTOCOL

AN ISLAND IN TIME

DOROTHY FITCH PENISTON

NO ORDINARY TIME

Franklin and Eleanor Roosevelt:
The Home Front in World War II

DORIS KEARNS GOODWIN

PRECEDING PAGES: Small oval rooms navigate irregular floor-plan geometries with grace. In the primary suite, a library acts as a traffic circle, connecting the primary bedroom, baths, and closets.

RIGHT: The upper lounge and gallery lead to the single guest suite in the main house. The lounge's balcony, overlooking the lagoon and the landscape, has the most dramatic view in the house.

ABOVE AND OPPOSITE: Sundown bougainvillea climbs the walls of the south-facing porch and veranda, reminding us we are in the subtropics.

OVERLEAF: The "long view," framed.

WINDSOR

SYMMETRY

S OMETIMES A PROJECT TAKES YOU PLACES YOU DON'T EXPECT. PETER expressed it well when he said, "This project has legs." And for whatever reason, it does. The recipient of a national Palladio Award and a regional Institute of Classical Architecture & Art Addison Mizner Award, this house has resonated with many people, including our own Moor Baker team, who chose it to grace the cover of *House Love* long before the book had been designed. But why? Its sculpted, gabled ends are quite striking, yes, but we think there is more to it. As romantics, we would venture to say that when a house has soul, it can be felt, and this house has it in spades. The design and construction teams were in harmony, led by our sophisticated and sure-footed clients. They charged us with designing a sensible, livable, pared-down home for their family, and the result lies squarely at the intersection of the three.

It so happens that the lot, overlooking a golf course, is situated at the southernmost end of the renowned New Urbanist community of Windsor in Vero Beach. We would be remiss not to express our gratitude for having Windsor in our own backyard. Its creation more than thirty years ago by DPZ CoDesign and the Weston family was intended as a sensible counterpoint to widespread suburban sprawl and clumsy attempts at Mediterranean-style architecture. Its gridded streets, lined with buildings reminiscent of such enduring Florida towns as St. Augustine, are people- and eco-friendly. Windsor leads by example to this day, with its North Village development demonstrating how to simultaneously develop and heal our land.

A familiar Vero Beach band was reunited for this project, with Sam Comer and Moor Baker teaming up on the landscaping, and Ashley Waddell and Courtney Harris of Olivia O'Bryan

designing the interiors, as they had for this family many times before. We all leaned hard into dramatic simplicity, the silver lining of a modest budget, skillfully executed by our friends at Indian River Masonry.

Our stint in Vermont taught us that our job is to find the local materials—and the methods of assembling them—that age gracefully. Windsor is a beach community, so in its ever-present sun and salt air, concrete and stucco reign supreme. As a result, we have watched our local concrete contractors hone their skills over the years, gradually becoming masters of what we call the liquid arts. They build intricate formwork in wood and fill it with concrete, creating durable, practical shapes intended to shed water or simply add delight. On more than one occasion, we have seen members of their team, and those of other trades, bring a spouse or a friend by the project to admire their own work. It turns out that house love is not just for those who end up living there.

PAGE 204: Initially intended merely to save space, this secondary, painted-concrete stair, which ascends to the two guest bedrooms, terminates the axis of the main entry gallery and is distinguished by its sculptural quality.

PAGES 206–7: On the rear façade, sculpted stucco both adds delight and serves useful functions in the form of twin gable ends, splays over windows, porch brackets, chimney caps, a raised pool coping, and privacy walls.

PRECEDING PAGES: This mid-block lot in the New Urbanist community of Windsor, planned by DPZ CoDesign, provided an opportunity to create a compact, axially symmetrical "garden villa" scheme in the spirit of Luytens and Palladio's much grander country estates.

OPPOSITE: A plaster dome illuminates the outdoor stairwell of the guesthouse. Overlooking the treetops in the courtyard below, its curved surface bends the light from above and below.

OVERLEAF: Garages flank the central axis, which extends all the way from the courtyard to the living spaces, the pool, and out to the pond, golf course, and woods.

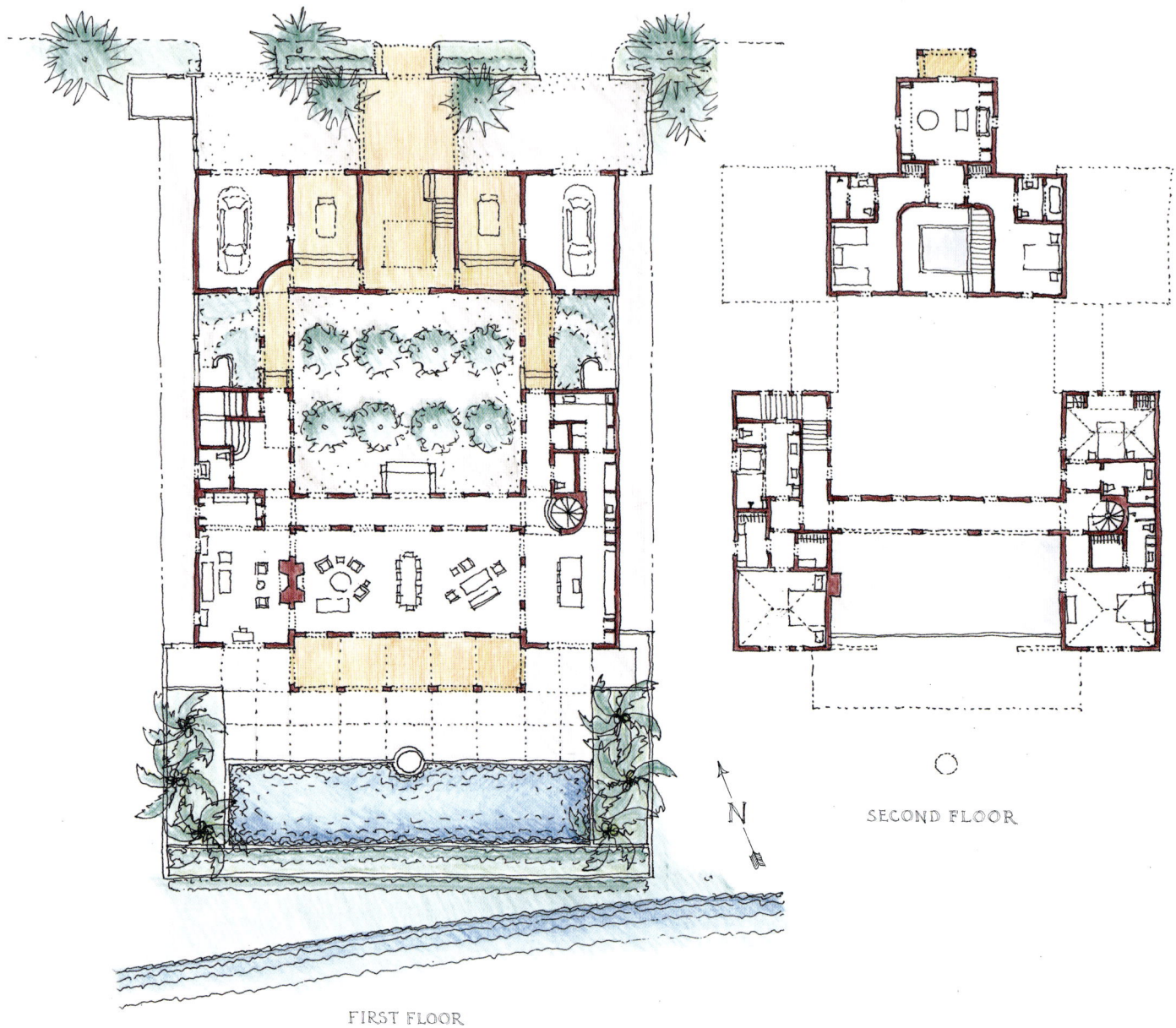

FIRST FLOOR

SECOND FLOOR

N

PAGES 214–15: The outdoor foyer leads to the courtyard and main house straight ahead, to the garage and cart storage on either side, and to the guest wing up the stairs.

PAGES 216–17: Eight native green buttonwood trees and four two-story walls define the central gravel courtyard, a cool retreat even on the hottest days.

PRECEDING PAGES: In this temperate microclimate, you can dine outdoors all year long. One of two outdoor showers can be seen beyond. One is for the pups and the other is for the humans.

OPPOSITE: At the base of the staircase to the primary suite, a series of tall, narrow windows admit abundant natural light. Polished concrete and drywall were used liberally; wood planking and Hope's steel windows were used sparingly, all a reflection of the clients' minimalist taste and sensible approach.

PAGES 222–23: The elegant spiral stair connects the guest bedrooms to the kitchen below.

PRECEDING PAGES: In the kitchen, tall cupboards, beautifully crafted by Premier, a local cabinet shop, house the dishes and the refrigerator. The top drawer of the cabinets overhangs the lower ones to accommodate long-footed fellows. A sheet of glass behind the cooktop makes cleanup easy and doesn't detract from the sculpted range hood or the handsome, counterweighted pendant.

OPPOSITE: Olivia O'Bryan, the family's longtime decorators, added dramatic lighting in several rooms, including this shimmering chandelier in the dining area of the double-height living space.

OVERLEAF: A double-sided fireplace separates the den from the double-height living area, which is overlooked by a glassed-in walkway connecting the primary and guest wings.

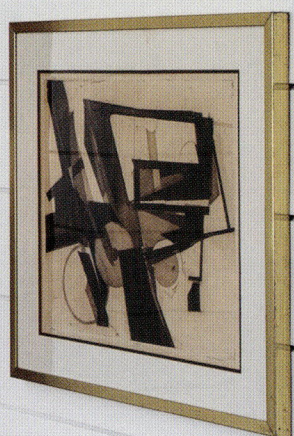

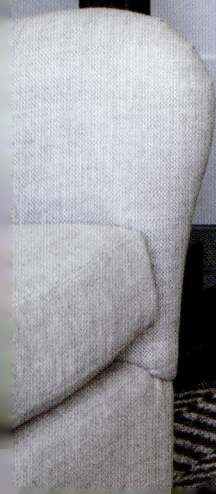

PAGES 230–31: An alcove in the den houses a library and a bar. Its moody palette can be appreciated from the den and from the front entry through an interior window.

PRECEDING PAGES: The den is decorated with art and objects collected over time.

OPPOSITE: Powder rooms often differ in style from the rest of the house. Here, an oversize pattern covers the walls, looking as though it was hand-drawn in situ.

OVERLEAF LEFT: We imagine stairs as pouring water, their energy expressed in how they spill out into a room. Here, treads softly wrap the corner, gently guiding you from the primary suite upstairs to the public spaces below.

OVERLEAF RIGHT: The top of the spiral stair, smartly lit by Olivia O'Bryan.

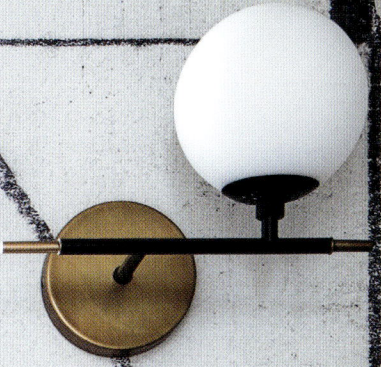

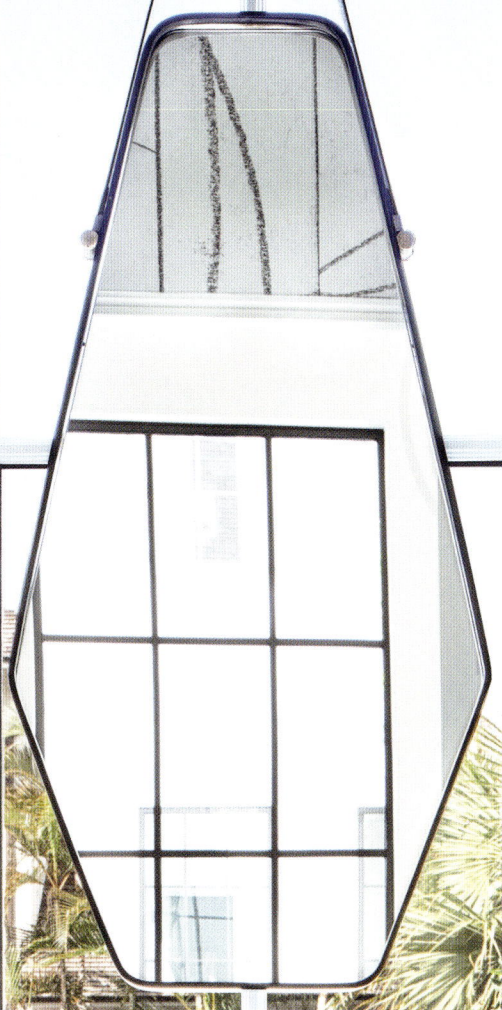

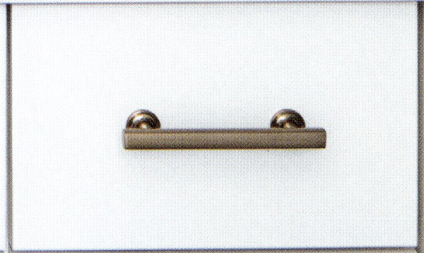

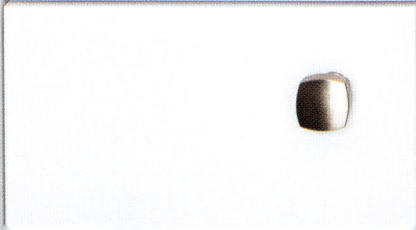

PRECEDING PAGES: The primary suite features a simple pitched ceiling and a window overlooking the backyard. With its soothing palette and soft textures, it provides a calm retreat from the rest of the house.

RIGHT: The well-appointed primary bathroom houses sundries in tall cabinets across from the soaking tub and shower. An expansive mirror over the double vanity brightens the room and makes it feel larger than it is.

ABOVE: One of the two gables on the rear façade reflects the late-day sun. The door below opens into the kitchen.

OPPOSITE: The pool stretches the length of the house and is visible from every room. Its coping is conveniently raised for sitting on, and a firepit at the center of the coping is on axis with the front door. On the wall at one end of the pool, espaliered Confederate jasmine vines have been trained into triangular "trees."

TAKE ME
TO THE
RIVER

SOMETIMES IT TAKES YEARS BEFORE A PROJECT'S IMPACT ON OUR firm's trajectory is fully realized, but in this case, we knew it immediately. It was 2009, and the Florida residential market was still very much in recession. As a result, Peter and I had plenty of time to reflect on our work, ourselves, and our clients, and to think about what we do best— our Why. We distilled it down to the architectural equivalent of portrait painting, with "bricks and mortar" as our medium, in the hope that our designs would reflect our clients' personalities, preferences, and taste, and instill in them the feeling that we have come to call "house love."

With so much extra time and so little extra cash, we decided to use our last few bucks on a party to celebrate the firm's upcoming anniversary. It was not a fancy party; we held it right in our small studio. We lined the walls with black display boards, on which we mounted images of our work in chronological order, starting with Vermont, and invited the whole town to come by. As luck would have it, the phone rang the following week with two new commissions, one of which was this project. We were back in business.

The magic of this lot quickly became obvious. Situated on the Indian River, it faces south, free from the harsh western sun common along this stretch of Vero Beach, and it was only a fifteen-minute walk from town. The place had soul. A charming midcentury house had occupied the site, its long, narrow structure raised up more than several feet, not far from the water's edge. As a result, it made us feel like we were standing on the deck of a boat. That was the feeling we sought to retain in our design of the new house, perhaps not consciously at first. We elevated the living spaces and situated the pool close to the building. The tall coping on the

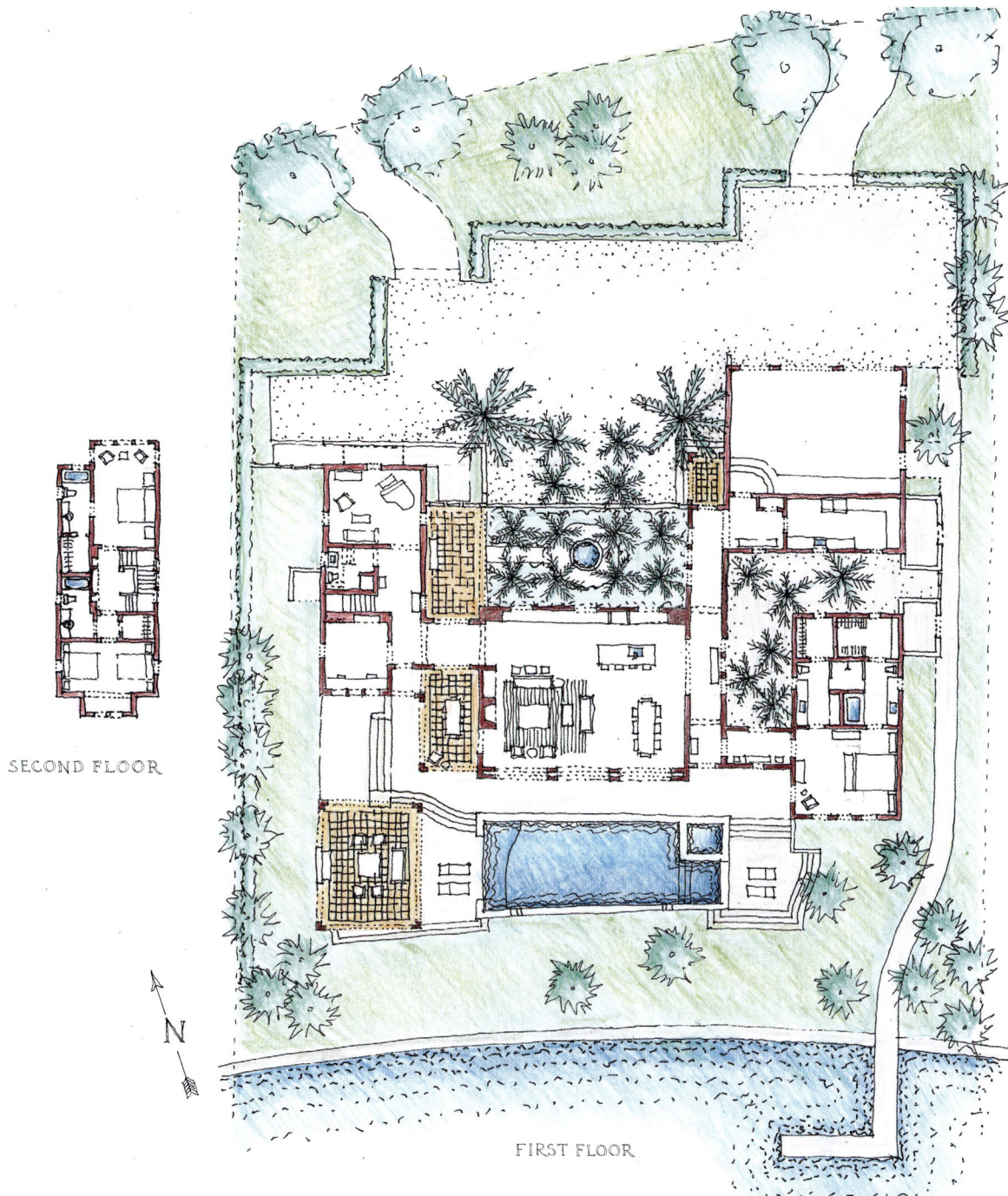

SECOND FLOOR

FIRST FLOOR

N

PAGE 244: Light filters dreamily into the potting porch, which overlooks the river and the bridge beyond. Marble pavers, stucco walls, and copper downspouts age gracefully.

PAGES 246–47: The street façade of the house's main pavilion overlooks a garden that is hidden behind a stucco wall topped by a profusion of Sundown bougainvillea. Parking spots in front of the wall are delineated by Christmas palms. The wings of the house are anchored by a pair of mature Medjool date palms.

PRECEDING PAGES: The modest front door is located in one of the wings.

OPPOSITE: The garden that is walled off from the street is surrounded on the other three sides by the entry hall, the kitchen, and the potting porch.

house side of the pool serves as a ha-ha wall, obscuring the pool from view when one is inside the house, so that the eye focuses on the sparkling river beyond.

We separated the interior spaces into four structures connected by glassy hallways. We filled the negative spaces with gardens that snake among the structures and connective hallways, the plantings almost appearing to be inside the rooms. The center structure is by far the tallest; its steel-framed openings are covered by a deep, sculptural overhang. A very wide hall connecting it to the practice room is commodious enough to wheel the piano back and forth for concerts.

The boatlike quality of this project remains. Stepping inside, you feel like you're floating above the twinkling river with Big Blue, our beloved, turquoise, midcentury power plant, off in the distance.

OPPOSITE: Tucked away down the hall from the kitchen, his office has one of the best views of the water.

OVERLEAF: The main living space consists of a long kitchen, a dining area, and a seating area. Raised above the surrounding grade, the space appears to be floating on the river just a few feet away.

PAGES 256–57: Gardens wrap around the property's structures, becoming an integral element of the interior décor, as seen in the dining area.

LEFT: Built into oak-paneled cabinetry by Shaver Millwork, the kitchen is located along the wall of the living space that faces the streetside courtyard.

ABOVE: Flanked by courtyard gardens, the hall leading from the front door to the river is bathed in natural light.

OPPOSITE: As seen in the vestibule of the primary suite, subtle moldings and polished-concrete floors provide a pristine backdrop for the owners' art collection and furniture, curated over time with their interior designers, Ashley Waddell and Courtney Harris of Olivia O'Bryan.

OPPOSITE: The roof of the pool cabana is made of staggered slats, which allow light and breezes in but keep the rain out.

OVERLEAF: Looking west toward the cabana, the main living space is on the right. The south-facing overhang shades the steel-framed windows and doors. Thick concrete tiles add dimension to the simple roof lines. From inside, the tall coping obscures the pool, so that the view is of the river, as if from the deck of a boat.

ON

THE

GREEN

W E HAVE SAID, IN JEST, THAT THIS IS OUR MOST SUCCESSFUL renovation. Although we were hired to renovate a rather new home in an established North Palm Beach community, we ended up saving—and, yes, successfully renovating—only the pool. When we first met our clients, introduced to us by their family decorators, Bierly Drake & Steele Inc., our task was to "improve the flow" and perhaps "move walls," but upon closer study, we realized that the structure of the house would prove impractical to renovate. During our first visit to the property, I recall how delighted we were to step out of the house and into the backyard, where we discovered the expansive view that was hardly visible from the interior. In the foreground was a gentle stream and, beyond it, rolling green hills, culminating in a surprise—urban towers hinting at a city in the distance. There was much to take in, and if you did so while inhaling deeply, you could catch a whiff of the nearby Atlantic. We were determined to take better advantage of this special place.

So, for our first presentation, we mustered a bit of courage and proposed a scheme for a completely new home. We employed a simplistic drawing, called a figure ground diagram, to illustrate the footprints of the existing and proposed houses side by side. In this abstracted form, the logic of the new plan and its connection of the indoors to the outdoors quickly became obvious. Our clients quietly listened to our proposal and then, to our relief, enthusiastically agreed.

The exterior was landscaped by our longtime collaborator, Mario Nievera. A master of scale, Nievera fearlessly fills the narrowest of planting beds with fronds of prehistoric scale. His

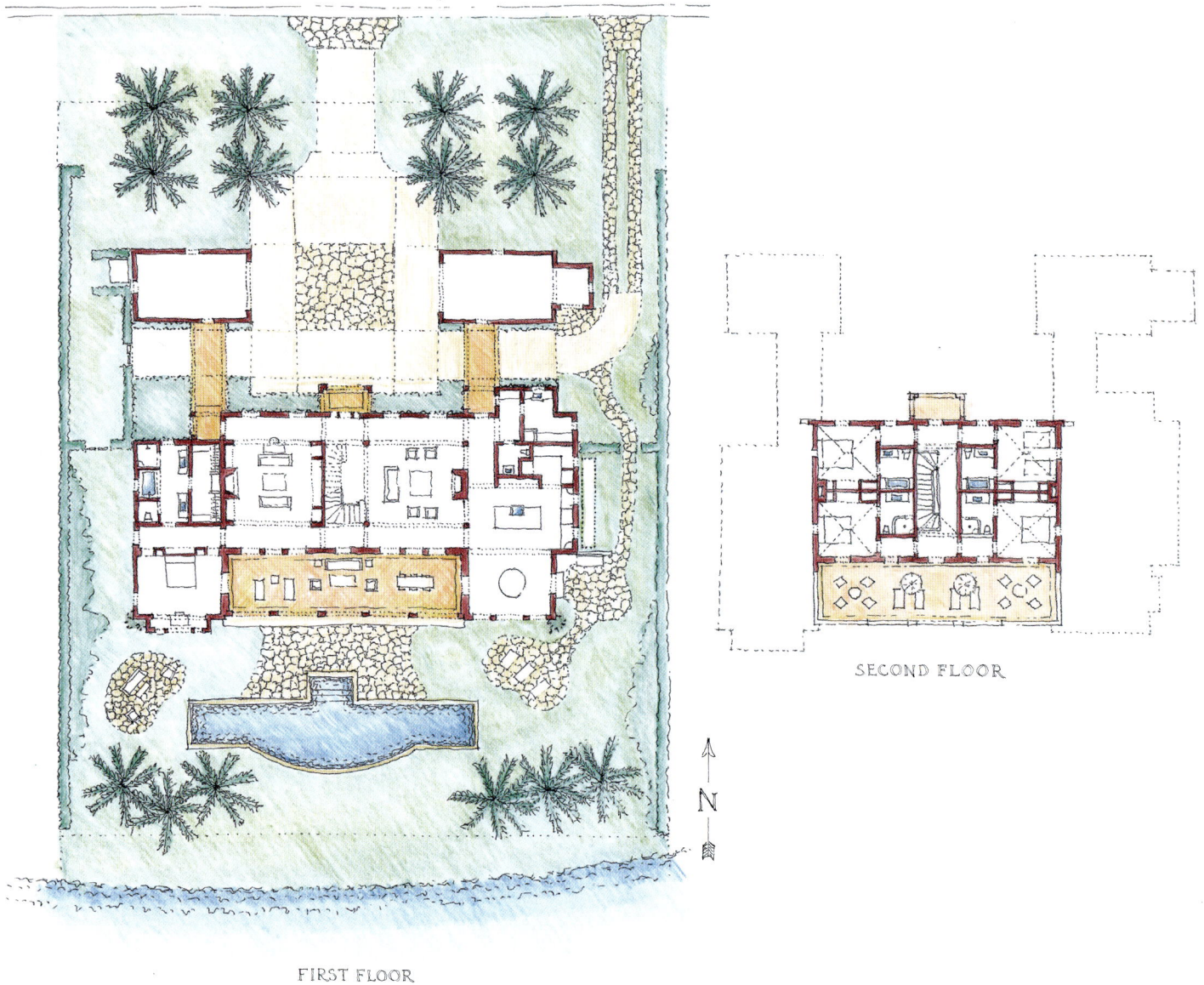

FIRST FLOOR

SECOND FLOOR

PAGE 266: A round window punctuates the stepped gable end of the single garages that flank the tabby concrete and coquina motor court.

PAGES 268–69: This Bermuda-style house is a response to its unique site features and idyllic setting. Its symmetrical two-story, five-bay, center hall plan is traditional.

PAGE 270: A stepped gable and lattice railings of painted brick top the center entry. The railings are inspired by the durable, low-maintenance terra-cotta railings seen in Palm Beach.

PRECEDING PAGES: His and her garages are detached but connected to the house by breezeways. The formal but friendly front door is on axis with the driveway.

OPPOSITE: In the center entry hall, a compact yet comfortable winding oak stair leads to four guest suites and the upper terrace.

compositions are somehow equal parts tailored and wild and always frame the architecture in ways that delight.

This place has become a refuge for the clients' growing family, with a gathering space large enough for all, and a respite for mom and dad when the house is in full swing. The kitchen, dining room, and living room are contiguous, but the primary suite is separated from those bustling spaces by a den. All the first-floor rooms open onto the twelve-foot-deep screened porch, which overlooks the view. Four tiny but mighty guest bedrooms occupy the four corners of the second floor, each a different color, and all have access to the upstairs terrace, perfect for cocktails under the stars. This is a home that many people can enjoy at the same time, whether together or away from the fray, all the while savoring the view across the green.

OPPOSITE: The upper stair hall culminates in the south terrace, with its sweeping view of the golf course.

OVERLEAF: A pair of living rooms flank the center entry hall. This one, located next to the primary suite, functions as a den to buffer the primary suite from the main living areas. Its doors can be closed, creating a respite for this husband and wife when there is a full house.

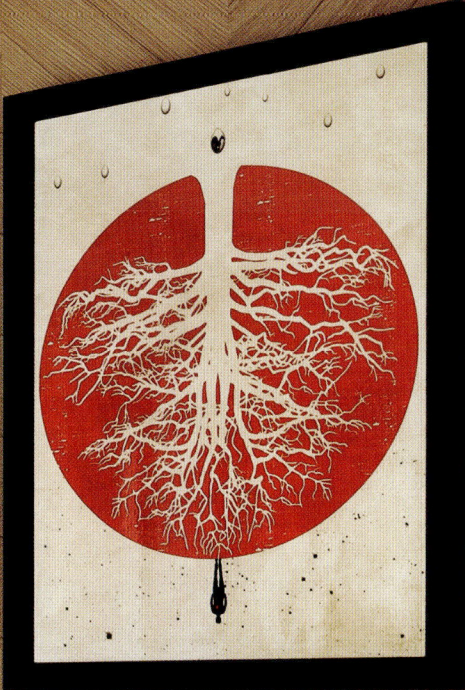

CHANEL N°5
at 100

ISLAND HOPPING
GRAY MALIN

LOUIS VUITTON
Louis Vuitton   Tambour

RALPH LAUREN
TOM SCHEERER MORE DECORATING

OPPOSITE AND ABOVE: The cabinetry in the den consists of oak planks with subtly eased edges. Notched sticks allow the shelf height to be adjusted—an old-school method. The fireplace surround is carved coral stone.

PRECEDING PAGES: A one-room-deep floor plan not only ensures that all spaces, including the family living room, are bathed in soft natural light from at least two sides but also brings the outdoors very much into each room.

OPPOSITE: The vented cabinetry of the heavily used family drop-off area can be seen in the shell-encrusted powder room mirror. The cantilevered marble sink appears to float, adding drama.

OPPOSITE AND ABOVE: The kitchen is open to the dining room on the right. The east wall features curved corner cupboards, handmade tiles, and a plaster range hood. Round columns bend the light and create a sense of separation from the family room.

OVERLEAF: The dining room feels as though it had once been an open porch. The large windows extend down to the coral-stone floors. The left and right windows can slide into pockets, opening the room to balmy breezes.

OPPOSITE: The primary suite anchors the west end of the house. The rooms are not large, but numerous built-ins make the cozy spaces feel spacious.

ABOVE: One of the four guest suites, each decorated differently.

OPPOSITE: The twelve-foot-deep porch facing the pool extends the entire length of the main living spaces, providing welcome shade. Pocket doors make the indoor-outdoor living easy.

ABOVE LEFT AND RIGHT: Mario Nievera's vision for the pool deck was simple and resort-like. Grass surrounds the coquina pool, irregularly shaped coral stone supports the lawn furniture, and palm fronds provide shade.

OVERLEAF: The south façade overlooks the golf course. The porch is flanked by the primary bedroom on the left and the dining room on the right. One-room deep, the floor plan enables most rooms to enjoy the view.

SKINNY
DIP

W E HAVE BEEN IN PRACTICE LONG ENOUGH TO HAVE DESIGNED a few homes for the children of our clients. Gaining multigenerational trust is a great privilege, but from time to time it has given us the impression that we can be bossier with the second generation. After spending a few minutes with this couple, however, that impression was summarily quashed. They exhibited not a bit of hesitation when it came to their vision for the project. Dedicated to their careers but longing for a respite, they desired a vacation home where they could work a little less while surrounded by things they love most—their growing collection of art, the sea, and each other's company.

They were quite fond of this Vero Beach neighborhood, having spent so much time at her parents' house down the street, and appreciated the integrity of the prevailing Georgian-style architecture in the community. They wanted their home to fit in but felt that a pared-down version of the houses typically built there would better suit their idea of a house and grounds as both a personal art gallery and a work of art in its own right. They knew we could make it comfortable and, as I recall, they admired her parents' home for being so well balanced and graceful, two important characteristics that transcend style. We were up to the task.

To give the property the dramatic ambiance of an art gallery, we designed an elaborate entrance sequence. Visitors approach through an allée of thin palms, arriving at a broad, lushly landscaped stair that ascends to a formidable garden gate. Beyond the gate, a long breezeway leads to the front door. To the right, stretching the entire length of the breezeway, is a lap pool, its surface mirroring the sky. At night, it glows. To the left is a sculpture garden, traversed by a

SECOND FLOOR

← N →

FIRST FLOOR

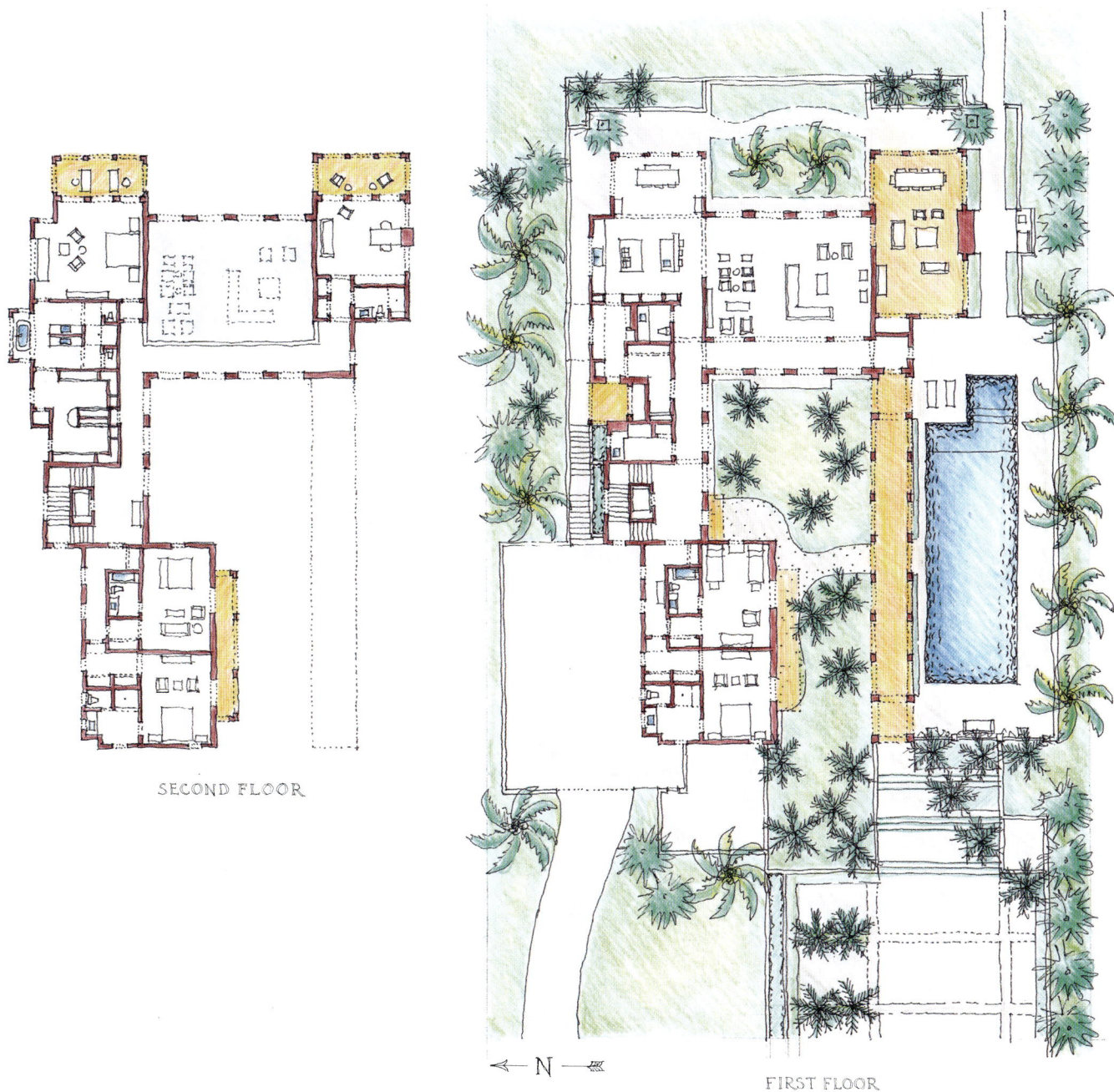

PAGE 296: The formal entry is reached through a long, colonnaded breezeway, minimal in its detailing. Parallel to it is the long lap pool, just out of sight to the right.

PAGES 298–99: A monumental stair to welcome guests is softened by layers of landscaping: beds of *Liriope* are punctuated by Christmas palms; creeping fig climbs the walls; and hedges of fuchsia bougainvillea explode with color.

PRECEDING PAGES: Thin palms shade the sculpture garden between the breezeway and the guest suites. The path is paved with native Florida caprock, a young limestone.

OPPOSITE: The rippling water of the lap pool is reflected on the ceiling of the breezeway.

path that leads to the guest suites. When visitors finally reach the front door, it opens to an entry niche, a pause before the breathtaking view of the Atlantic Ocean is revealed just around a corner.

The materials are rich. A combination of rustic oyster stone and refined French limestone is used for the flooring. Drop shiplap siding, typically used outdoors, wraps the walls of the main living space—a nod to coastal tradition. Its grooved surface bends the light and, painted a high-gloss, creamy white, it brightens the room. Here, as throughout the house, subtle moldings and creamy white walls provide a pristine backdrop for the couple's impressive and ever-growing art collection.

The predominant accent color, cleverly chosen by the interior design team at Smythe & Cortlandt, is a cheerful tangerine. A perfect foil to the sapphire-blue ocean, it is used on the shutters in the open-air cabana at the ocean end of the pool and appears in a highly lacquered version on the kitchen ceiling.

The primary suite and the couple's office are located on the second floor. The passage between them, a glass-lined gallery, floats over the double-height living space.

Like the interior, the exterior, with its simple white concrete roof, its walls covered in the soft glow of white mineral paint, and its symmetrically placed doors and windows, serves as a backdrop for art, but in this case the art is the lush Floridian landscape. Lime-green palm fronds, blue skies, occasional pelicans overhead, and gardens punctuated with fuchsia bougainvillea hedges—the leaves of which, almost electric in color, drift poetically to the ground—steal the show.

This stretch of Florida holds a quiet magic that we have enjoyed sharing with families lucky enough to find it, this couple among them. They were willing to put their trust in us in this paradise, and the result is a sublime haven filled with house love.

OPPOSITE: The walls of the double-height main living space are clad in gloss-painted shiplap siding. Just beyond is the kitchen. The upstairs gallery, running along the west side between the primary bedroom and the home office, enjoys a magnificent view of the ocean.

OVERLEAF: A double-height wall of windows and doors seemingly brings sky, sea, and coconut palms right into the living space.

PAGE 308: The dining room looks as though it was originally a porch that was later enclosed with glass.

PAGE 309: Minimal Italian cabinetry by Poliform wraps the kitchen. The cooktop overlooks the gardens below. The lacquered tangerine ceiling reflects the light streaming in from the windows, brightening the space.

PAGES 310–11: In the open-air cabana, shutters frame the view of the Atlantic, modulate prevailing breezes, and keep out the occasional rain.

PRECEDING PAGES: Coconut palms and native sabal palms front the view of the dunes and the ocean from the cabana.

OPPOSITE: The cabana buffers the pool from the ocean but does not block it. To the left, the colonnaded breezeway parallels the long lap pool, a nonnegotiable requirement of our client, who is an avid swimmer.

OVERLEAF: The house becomes a lantern in the evening, its soft glow reflected in the pool.

PROJECT CREDITS

All exterior and interior architecture is by Moor Baker Architects, in collaboration with the talented individuals and teams listed below.

LESSONS FROM VERMONT
Residence, Page 17
Builder: Hammer Time Construction Inc.
   with W J Homolka Cabinetry & Furniture
Interior Design (not shown): Owner

OUR HOUSE
Builder: RCL Development, Inc.
Interior Design: Peter Moor and Mary Juckiewicz
Landscape Design: Sam Comer of Hayslip Landscape

PRETTY IN PINK
Builder: Tim Givens Building & Remodeling Inc.
Interior Design: Tom Scheerer of Tom Scheerer, Inc.
Landscape Design: Mario Nievera of Nievera Williams
   Landscape Architecture

HORSE PLAY
Builder: Gast Construction Group, Inc.
Interior Design: Tom Scheerer of Tom Scheerer, Inc.
Landscape Design: Mario Nievera of Nievera Williams
   Landscape Architecture

SHORE BIRD
Builder: Barth Construction, Inc.
Interior Design: Owner
Landscape Design: Sam Comer of Hayslip Landscape

UNDER THE OAKS
Builder: Wissel Construction, Inc.
Interior Design: Owner
Landscape Design: Sam Comer of Hayslip Landscape

GOOD NEIGHBOR
Builder: Barth Construction, Inc.
Interior Staging: Hazel House
Landscape Design: Jane McBride of Down to Earth
   Landscape & Irrigation

THE LONG VIEW
Builder: Croom Construction Company
Interior Design: Lee Bierly and Christopher Drake of
   Bierly Drake & Steele, Inc.
Landscape Design: Elizabeth A. Gillick of Elizabeth
   A. Gillick, Inc.

WINDSOR SYMMETRY
Builder: Barth Construction, Inc.
Interior Design: Ashley Waddell and Courtney Harris
   of Olivia O'Bryan Inc.
Landscape Design: Sam Comer of Hayslip Landscape

TAKE ME TO THE RIVER
Builder: Barth Construction, Inc.
Interior Design: Ashley Waddell and Courtney Harris
   of Olivia O'Bryan, Inc.
Landscape Design: Sam Comer of Hayslip Landscape

ON THE GREEN
Builder: Webb Builders, LLC
Interior Design: Christopher Drake and William Steele
   of Bierly Drake & Steele, Inc.
Landscape Design: Mario Nievera of Nievera Williams
   Landscape Architecture

SKINNY DIP
Builder: The Hill Group
Interior Design: Anthony Tinghitella and John Fulcher
   of Smythe & Cortlandt
Landscape Design: Sam Comer of Hayslip Landscape

ACKNOWLEDGMENTS

Architecture is perhaps the most cumbersome of the arts and requires a veritable army of dedicated souls. We are grateful for all of them.

Our list must begin with our clients. Their trust, patience, and belief in us to design the house they envision in their mind's eye makes every day worthwhile.

Our dedicated team, who have contributed their time, talents, and a good deal of patience to the creation of *House Love* within our studio walls. It takes a village.

Jessica Klewicki Glynn, our gimlet-eyed photographer, who suggested the idea of a book to Mark Magowan of Vendome and has beautifully documented most of our projects over the years, continually delights us with images that capture the spirit of our work. Working with Vendome has been a pleasure. The elegant guidance from publisher Mark Magowan, editor Jackie Decter, and book designer Rita Sowins has helped us see our work with fresh eyes.

None of this would be possible without a multitude of collaborators and colleagues, including builders, craftspeople, interior designers, landscape designers, and suppliers of building products and materials, as well as the inspiration we derive from professional organizations, especially the Institute of Classical Architecture & Art.

PETER MOOR, MARY JUCKIEWICZ, & CHRIS BAKER

Our team, *FROM LEFT:* Chris Baker (Principal Architect), Page Wallace (Office Manager), Regyne Heurtelou (Design Associate), Peter Moor (Founding Principal Architect) with Lily (the office pup), Norm Kennedy (Senior Associate), Shannar O'Connor (Design Associate), Kiera Tucker (Design Associate), and Mary Juckiewicz (Founding Architect)

House Love
First published in 2025 by The Vendome Press
Vendome is a registered trademark of The Vendome Press LLC

VENDOME PRESS US
PO Box 566
Palm Beach, FL 33480

VENDOME PRESS UK
Worlds End Studio
132–134 Lots Road
London SW10 0RJ

www.vendomepress.com

ISBN: 978-0-86565-466-2

PUBLISHERS: Beatrice Vincenzini, Mark Magowan, and Francesco Venturi

EDITOR: Jacqueline Decter
PRODUCTION MANAGER: Amanda Mackie
PRODUCTION DIRECTOR: Jim Spivey
DESIGNER: Rita Sowins / Sowins Design
ILLUSTRATOR: Peter Moor

Library of Congress Cataloging-in-Publication Data available upon request

Distributed in North America by:
Abrams Books
www.abramsbooks.com

Distributed in the rest of the world by:
Thames & Hudson Ltd.
6–24 Britannia Street
London WC1X 9JD
United Kingdom
www.thamesandhudson.com

EU Authorized Representative:
Interart S.A.R.L.
19 Rue Charles Auray
93500 Pantin, Paris
France
productsafety@vendomepress.com
www.interart.fr

Printed and bound in China by RR Donnelley (Guangdong) Printing Solutions

First printing

PHOTO CREDITS

All photos by © Jessica Klewicki Glynn, with the exception of the following:
© Alan Karchmer: 10
© Arthur Tilley: 16
Client: 17
© Jacqui Cole: 38 left

PAGES 2–3: Located in the beachside community of Windsor, Florida, this residence presented a rare opportunity for symmetry amid predominantly side-yard houses. We took advantage of it, adding a pair of sculpted gable ends that bookend a colonnade of elongated ogee brackets, all formed and poured by our talented local concrete artisans. The graceful shapes and curves stand out against the cedar-shingle roof. "Tropical Hogwarts" is what we affectionately call our riff on this Anglo-Caribbean house.

PAGES 4–5: We refer to this room in a Vero Beach, Florida, house as the "save-some-pecky-for-the-rest-of-us" room. The walls and most of the ceilings in the home are clad in pecky cypress. We began to paint it but stopped after the first coat of primer, enjoying its natural warmth.

PAGES 6–7: This true sleeping porch on the second floor of a home in Palm Beach is elevated above the bustling street corner below and has a sweeping view of the dunes and the Atlantic Ocean beyond.

PAGE 8: Alfresco meals in Florida are possible all year-round. This outdoor room remains cool even on the hottest days, shaded by the native green buttonwoods and cooled by the breezes that waft though various openings.

PAGE 10: A welcoming entrance fronts the street. Stucco, mahogany, and an exposed metal roof frame the enfilade of arches through the house and offer a glimpse of the golf course beyond.

PAGES 12–13: With its soaring ceiling diminished in scale by clever layering of beams, moldings, and furnishings, this room invites you to grab a book, light a fire, and stay a while.